IF MY PEOPLE

A Call to the Church

A study in the revelation and application of an Old Testament truth to the New Testament Church and the believers who form it.

Courtney A. Laird

If My People
A Call to the Church
Copyright © – Courtney Laird – 2019

ISBN:978-0-6488463-0-7

All rights reserved. No part of this publication may be reproduced, stored in a retrieval system, or transmitted in any form or by any means mechanical, electronic, photocopying, recording or otherwise without the express written permission of the author.

The author can be contacted at:
courtney.a.laird@gmail.com

All scripture references, unless otherwise indicated, are taken from the Authorised King James version of the Bible.

Words of scripture written in bold are used by the writer for specific emphasis

DEDICATION

To my amazing wife who blessed me with the time to form and write this study and looked after our three delightful children while I did so. Thank you for your patience and support in this endeavour. I love you.

To Kevin Conner a father and mentor in the faith who equipped me with the tools to be able to write this. I will be forever grateful for your input into my life.

PREFACE

The basis of this study was birthed in the writer's heart in October/November of 2019. In the time taken to compile, edit and format the text much changed in the world. The coronavirus pandemic hit and impacted the world on an unprecedented scale. Few could have imagined the impact this would have on a worldwide scale.

Within the pages of this study one of the topics that we cover is the judgement of the Lord. As we do so the reader may well see some correlation between the points made and the state of things today. Whilst the Lord's judgment is discussed throughout, the premise of this study was not built upon such.

The title of this study, "If My People", is a quote from 2 Chronicles 7:14 where the Lord addresses the nation of Israel. This study is written with a call and a message to spiritual Israel, the Church. The heart of the writer, and indeed what he has felt be the heart of the Lord through this, is a call to the people of the Lord to seek Him with a fresh fervency and vigour. It is the writer's prayer that the reader will be able to hear the message of the Lord within these pages.

Blessings in Christ.

Courtney A. Laird.

CONTENTS

DEDICATION iii
PREFACE v
STUDY INTRODUCTION 1

PART A: RETURNING TO BLESSING 3
   SECTION INTRODUCTION 5
   EXPOSITION 7
   EXPOSITION SUMMARY 27
   EXAMPLE 29
   EXAMPLE SUMMARY 41
   SUMMARY OF EXPOSITION AND EXAMPLE 43
   APPLICATION 47
   APPLICATON SUMMARY 71
   SUMMARY OF EXPOSITION, EXAMPLE AND APPLICATION ... 73
   CONCLUSION 77
   THE CALL TO THE CHURCH 79

PART B: REMAINING IN BLESSING 83
   SECTION INTRODUCTION 85
   CONTINUATION 87
   CONTINUATION SUMMARY 117
   SUPPLEMENTAL A 123
   SUPPLEMENTAL B 127
   FINAL REMARKS 129

PART C: CHARTS & TABLES 131
   THE CHOSEN PLACE 133
   THE JUDGEMENTS 134
   THE BLESSINGS 134
   SPIRITUAL INCLINE 135
   SPIRITUAL DECLINE 135
   TAKE HEED 136
   COMBINATION 137

STUDY INTRODUCTION

If my people, which are called by my name, shall humble themselves, and pray, and seek my face, and turn from their wicked ways; then will I hear from heaven, and will forgive their sin, and will heal their land. (2Ch 7:14)

In late 2019 my wife and I were in a time of prayer and fasting. During this time we had decided to watch several sermons that we had on DVD. One of the ones we listened to was by Wendel Smith and in it he mentioned, just briefly, the above verse from 2 Chronicles.

Whilst the mention was brief it was one of those occurrences where the verse was quickened to the writer's heart. It was in meditating upon this verse that the writer's heart was stirred by the Lord to study this verse and its surrounding passages. What has come from that forms the basis of this short study. It is the writer's belief that there is a renewed call of the Lord in these latter days for the people of God and the Church, not just in Australia, but worldwide, to understand the truths of this verse and how they apply to us. It was in meditating upon this thought that the writer was also prompted on Ezekiel 22 30:

> *And I sought for a man among them, that should make up the hedge, and stand in the gap before me for the land, that I should not destroy it: but I found none. (Eze 22:30)*

The call of the Lord is for His people and His Church to apply the truths of 2 Chronicles 7:14 and stand in the gap, united as the body of Christ, for the nations that we live in.

This study is broken into two parts. Part A is called Returning to Blessing and in this we will look at three sections: Exposition, Example and Application. Part B is entitled Remaining in Blessing and here we will consider our fourth section of this study called Continuation.

Whilst our focus for this study starts in 2 Chronicles 7, we will follow the truths we discover here through the Word of God. It is the writer's prayer that he can accurately communicate and articulate that which the Lord has placed on his heart and that the reader will be able to glean the truths the Lord is wanting to communicate to His people

PART A: RETURNING TO BLESSING

SECTION INTRODUCTION

In Part A of our study we are going to look at three distinct sections of Exposition, Example and Application. Our purpose here is to discover the truths revealed to us in scripture before seeing them exemplified in the Word and then finally closing with a consideration of their application to believers and the Church of today. As we consider each of these sections, we will hopefully form a threefold witness that agrees with the truths we have discovered.

As we step through these sections the writer has endeavoured to keep the format the same so that the reader can see the progression of truth and revelation in each section. This format should allow the reader to easily flip between sections to compare and contrast the various points being made.

Finally, we will close this section with a summation of what the writer believes the Lord has placed on his heart as the study formed and progressed. It is the writer's belief that there is a clear message of the Lord in this for the Church today.

EXPOSITION

Unlocking the scriptural truths of 2 Chronicles 7

The focus of this section is on 2 Chronicles 7:11-16 which is quoted in full below. This passage forms the basis from which the rest of this study flows. This was the first piece of the puzzle, if you will, that the Lord spoke to the writer about. It was through studying and meditating upon the words of the Lord here that the Lord prompted the writer on other passages to search out. As the writer followed the leading of the Lord, the pieces came together and the study formed. The greatest revealer of scriptural truths is the Lord and He does that as we press in and seek Him for it. The reader is likewise encouraged to read, re-read and meditate upon these verses before moving on with the study.

Thus Solomon finished the house of the LORD, and the king's house: and all that came into Solomon's heart to make in the house of the LORD, and in his own house, he prosperously effected. (12) And the LORD appeared to Solomon by night, and said unto him, I have heard thy prayer, and have chosen this place to myself for an house of sacrifice. (13) If I shut up heaven that there be no rain, or if I command the locusts to devour the land, or if I send pestilence among my people; (14) If my people, which are called by my name, shall humble themselves, and pray, and seek my face, and turn from their wicked ways; then will I hear from heaven, and will forgive their sin, and will heal their land. (15) Now mine eyes shall be open, and mine ears attent unto the prayer that is made in this place. (16) For now have I chosen and sanctified this house, that my name may be there for ever: and mine eyes and mine heart shall be there perpetually. (2Ch 7:11-16)

This passage centres on the Lord revealing Himself to Solomon and communicating with him through a dream. Here the Lord appears to Solomon and responds to Solomon's prayer as recorded in 1 Kings 8 and 2 Chronicles 6. Within this discourse of the Lord there are five points for us to consider. These are:

A. The Chosen Place
B. The Judgements
C. The People
D. The Response
E. The Promise

These five points will correspond throughout the first three sections of this study as we look at our sections of Exposition, Example and Application. As we progress through this study and build upon these points, the truths that these five points have to the people of

Exposition

God and the Church should become evident. For now, let us move into our exposition of 2 Chronicles 7.

A. <u>The Chosen Place</u>
And the LORD appeared to Solomon by night, and said unto him, I have heard thy prayer, and have chosen this place to myself for an house of sacrifice. (2Ch 7:12)

The Lord appeared to Solomon in a dream by night and outlined three things:

1. I have heard thy prayer
2. I have chosen this place
3. This place is to be a house of sacrifice

The central piece in each of these three points is the chosen place. The chosen place was where Solomon's prayer was heard, and the chosen place was to be a house of sacrifice. Both of these points have at their centre the chosen place. Before we can consider points one and three we first need to look at what the chosen place was and what it reveals to us.

1. The Place
What is the chosen place? In verse 12 and verse 16 of 2 Chronicles 7 we see the word 'chosen' used by the Lord:

> *And the LORD appeared to Solomon by night, and said unto him, I have heard thy prayer, **and have chosen this place** to myself for an house of sacrifice. (2Ch 7:12)*
>
> ***For now have I chosen and sanctified this house**, that my name may be there for ever: and mine eyes and mine heart shall be there perpetually. (2Ch 7:16)*

The Lord refers to this place as His chosen place and His chosen and sanctified House. If we look back a little, we discover that from 2 Chronicles Chapter 2 to Chapter 8, the focus of scripture is on the Temple of Solomon and that is exactly what the Lord is referring to here. The chosen place and the chosen and sanctified house are the Temple of Solomon.

The Temple of Solomon was the third tabernacle/temple structure recorded in scripture. In order of Biblical revelation, we have the Tabernacle of Moses, the Tabernacle of David and finally the Temple of Solomon. All of these structures were built according to the Word of the Lord and all carry much truth applicable to the Church and believers today. Our purpose here is not to divulge into this but rather look at the implications of the Temple of Solomon as the chosen place.

The Temple of Solomon was actually born in the heart of David, but David was not the one the Lord would have to build it. David prepared as much as he could for the building and then handed things over to his son Solomon. David had the desire to build a permanent house for the Lord but it was Solomon who would accomplish this feat. The focus of the first several books of 2 Chronicles centres around Solomon's preparations for the building of the temple, the actual building of the temple and finally the dedication of the Temple of the Lord.

It is after Solomon has completed this project and indeed after the dedication of the Temple, that we arrive in 2 Chronicles 7 and read of the Lord having chosen the Temple. As we have seen above the Lord emphatically announces twice that He has chosen and sanctified this house/place. The Lord has looked upon and chosen this place. What caught the writer's mind was the language used here in the King James version of the Bible. The Lord specifically states that He has chosen, that is, it is something that has already been accomplished. He is not choosing it, He has already chosen it. The choice has already occurred. The Hebrew word used in vs 12 and 16 for chosen is "bachar" and according to The Englishmen's Hebrew Concordance of the Old Testament in these two passages it is used in the tense referred to as "preterite". The preterite, also called perfect, tense expresses an action that is complete or one that is perceived to have been completed. It is essentially something that has already been accomplished.

The Lord here isn't saying that He is choosing the Temple of Solomon, He is saying that He has already done it. The chosen place is a completed action, it has already occurred and the Lord here is pointing back to that. Verse 12 in particular indicates that this choice happened shortly after the Lord had heard Solomon's prayer:

> ...., *I have heard thy prayer,* **and have chosen this place** *to Myself for an house of sacrifice (2Ch 7:12)*

The question that arose in the writer's mind is what signified that the Temple of Solomon was indeed chosen by the Lord? Why was the Lord emphatic about having chosen the Temple and what was the indication that this had been done? What had signified the choice of the Lord?

In answer to this the writer was directed back to the start of 2 Chronicles 7 and it is here that we see the linkage between Solomon's prayer and the Lord's demonstration that He had chosen the Temple of Solomon.

> *Now when Solomon* ***had made an end of praying, the fire came down from heaven,*** *and consumed the burnt offering and the sacrifices;* ***and the glory of the LORD filled the house.*** *(2) And the priests could not enter into the house of the LORD, because the glory of the LORD had filled the LORD'S house. (3) And when all the children of Israel saw* ***how the fire came down, and the glory of the LORD upon the house,*** *they bowed themselves with their faces to the ground*

Exposition

upon the pavement, and worshipped, and praised the LORD, saying, For he is good; for his mercy endureth for ever. (2Ch 7:1-3)

In 2 Chronicles 6 we read that Solomon knelt before the Lord in worship upon a brazen scaffold he had made and offered a prayer of dedication unto the Lord. Then as we get in to Chapter 7 we read that when Solomon had made an end of praying that fire came down from the Lord and consumed the sacrifices that were upon the altar and the glory of the Lord filled the house. How incredible this must have been to witness, to see the literal fire of the Lord fall from heaven to earth and to see His glory fill this man made Temple. It must have been incredibly humbling and must have produced much Godly fear.

The fire of the Lord falls in both judgement and blessing. Throughout scripture, whenever the fire of the Lord consumes a sacrifice that is offered it is a fire of blessing and acceptance. Consider the following:

a) In Judges 6 Gideon's sacrifice was shown to be accepted when the angel of the Lord extended his staff and the sacrifice was consumed by fire that rose from the rock.

b) At the dedication of the Tabernacle of Moses the fire of the Lord came out from the Most Holy Place and consumed the sacrifices upon the brazen altar, showing the Lord's acceptance and choice of the Tabernacle system (Lev 9:24)

c) At the end of his time on earth the prophet Elijah was taken up by a chariot of fire and horses of fire in a whirlwind to heaven. The Lord had chosen and accepted him as a living sacrifice. (2 Kings 2:11).

The fire of the Lord signified that the Lord had accepted the sacrifice and was well pleased with it. It is this fire of blessing that signified that the Lord had chosen the Temple of Solomon. It was found acceptable in the Lord's sight and this was demonstrated through the provision of heavenly fire. Consider the verse comparison:

*Now when Solomon **had made an end of praying, the fire came down from heaven,** (2 Ch 7:1)*

*....., **I have heard thy prayer, and have chosen this place** to myself for an house of sacrifice (2Ch 7:12)*

Solomon's Perspective	**The Lord's Perspective**
2 Chronicles 7:1	2 Chronicles 7:12
Solomon finishes praying	I have heard thy prayer
Solomon sees the fire come down	I have Chosen

The choice of the Lord and the Lord's fire are one and the same thing. The chosen place was demonstrated, confirmed and attested to by the fire of the Lord. It is the fire that signifies the Temple of Solomon as the Lord's chosen place. The Lord's choice and the Lord's fire (in blessing) are linked. They are one and the same.

The Lord declares His chosen place through the provision of His Holy fire. It was His Holy fire of blessing that signified His acceptance and choice of the chosen place.

2.   The Place of Heard Prayer
I have heard thy prayer. (2 Ch 7:12)

The chosen place is the place of heard prayer. It was in the chosen place that the Lord heard the prayer of Solomon detailed for us in 2 Chronicles 6. In this prayer Solomon presents a number of scenarios to the Lord focusing on the Temple of Solomon and prayer made at or toward it. The Lord takes this prayer of Solomon in verses 14-42 and simply says I have heard thy prayer. Solomon was left with absolutely no doubt that the petitions he had brought to the Lord had been heard. The Lord had heard the prayer of Solomon at the chosen place. There is a link between the chosen place and heard prayer. The two are interconnected.

3.   The Place of Sacrifice
have chosen this place to myself for an house of sacrifice (2 Ch 7:12)

The Lord had chosen the Temple of Solomon. He had heard the prayer of Solomon made there. He then says that He has chosen this place to be a house of sacrifice. The chosen place was to be a house of sacrifice. Throughout the Old Testament the Lord had set places for where His sacrifices were to be offered. This truth is best evidenced with the Tabernacle of Moses where the Lord clearly outlines to the nation of Israel how sacrifice was to work and where and how it was to be offered. The Lord here takes that truth and applies it to the temple of Solomon. The Temple of Solomon as the chosen place was to be the place where sacrifice occurred. The chosen place was a place of sacrifice.

From verse 12 we have seen the Lord speak about the chosen place, the fact that He heard the prayer of Solomon and the fact that the chosen place was to be a place of sacrifice. Just as the chosen place and prayer are linked so too are the chosen place and sacrifice. In actual fact these three elements of the chosen place, heard prayer and sacrifice are all interlinked and this is the truth that we see with the Temple of Solomon. The chosen place is the choice of the Lord and it is here that He hears the prayer of His saints and it is here where sacrifice is to be made. Once the Lord has designated His choice through the provision of His Holy fire, the other two naturally follow The chosen place is be a place of prayer and sacrifice.

Exposition

B. The Judgements

We move now to the next part of our exposition which focuses on the judgements of the Lord as revealed to us in 2 Chronicles 7:13:

> *If I shut up heaven that there be no rain, or if I command the locusts to devour the land, or if I send pestilence among my people; (2Ch 7:13)*

In the above verse we observe that the Lord lists three judgements that He may perform. In I Kings 8 and 2 Chronicles 6 Solomon presents his prayer of dedication to the Lord and in it he outlines seven judgements of the Lord. He then asks for the Lord's mercy concerning these if the people return to the House of the Lord (the chosen place) and seek Him. The Lord takes these seven judgements of Solomon and condenses them down to three.

The requests of Solomon centred around the people of the Lord seeking the Lord at the chosen place in times of need and when they had wandered away from the Lord. Solomon outlines his concerns and also how he thought the Lord would react. The Lord takes these concerns of Solomon and in a simplified version says that if my people wander from me, this is how I will react. The Lord gives His people advance notice of what His judgments are so that the judgements may act as an early warning system to His people giving them the opportunity to repent and correct their path.

The Lord here lists three judgements that may proceed from Him as drought, locusts and pestilence. As we take a look at the effects of each of these it is interesting to note that the Lord uses different language when talking about each judgement. As we look through these judgements it will also be seen that they are progressive in nature, with each subsequent judgement building upon the previous.

1. Drought – Judgement 1
If I shut up the heaven that there be no rain (2Ch 7:13)

If the Lord shuts up the heavens. To have a shut heaven means that there is to be no rain. It is the closing of the skies and prohibiting of clouds pouring out rain upon the land.

It is the Lord who controls the store house of rain. Drought, no rain, can be a judgement from the Lord. Rain is a blessing from God for the earth (Heb 6:7). When a nation turns it's back on the Lord this blessing can be removed. Rain is something that can be taken for granted and it is only when it is removed that we truly value the blessing that it is.

Rain and water are a necessity for life on earth. Man and animals cannot live without water. In recognition of this man builds dams and water storages to be able to store large amounts of water in order to have a safety net when things dry up. Man understands the need of water. When the Lord shuts the heavens the resources of man eventually get stretched and we start to become aware of the direness of the situation. Man though is not the only one impacted by drought.

Hebrews 6:7 not only tells us that rain is a blessing it also tells us that the earth uses the rain to bring forth food for man.

> *For the earth which drinketh in the rain that cometh oft upon it, and bringeth forth herbs meet for them by whom it is dressed, receiveth blessing from God: (Heb 6:7)*

Drought affects man, it affects the food he is able to produce from the earth and it also impacts the animals he may raise for meat. When the heavens are shut the natural production abilities of the earth start to be diminished. Production decreases and scarcity increases. What starts as drought sets a course towards famine. Ultimately drought affects the ability for life to be sustained and birthed on the earth. Drought affects life in the human kingdom, the plant kingdom and the animal kingdom. When rain is withheld life diminishes. When rain returns life is birthed. How quickly does the grass turn green and fresh shoots appear when a drought stricken land receives the blessing of rain? When the heavens are shut though, rain is halted, drought ensues and life is affected. Drought affects life. This is the first judgement of the Lord

2. Locusts devouring
If I command the locusts to devour the land (2Ch 7:13)

The second judgment of the Lord is that He will command locusts to devour the land. A locust is a winged insect of the grasshopper family and is usually a solitary creature. They do however have a swarming phase and locusts, whilst small, can cause great destruction when large numbers congregate depleting crops and vegetation.

In this passage we see that it is a spoken command by the Lord for the locusts to act.

> *If I **command** the locusts to devour the land*

The Lord commands the locusts to act. The heavens being shut is an action. The command to the locusts is a spoken ordinance by the Lord.

Throughout the scriptures the locusts appear as a creature linked to plagues that strip the land of vegetation.

a) In Exodus 10:12 we see that a plague of locusts came from the Lord against the land of Egypt. It states here that they would eat every herb of the land that had been left by the hail. The plague of hail had destroyed the crops and the locusts would finish the rest.

Exposition

    b)   Judges 6:5 we see the armies of Midian compared to grasshoppers. This is the same root word for locusts. The Midianites literally swarmed in and encamped on the land of Israel. In verse 4 it tells us that they destroyed the increase of the earth and left no sustenance for Israel. The nation was greatly impoverished because of this and hope was taken from the people of the Lord.

Locusts are a plague sent by the Lord, at His command, to strip the land of what life has been produced. It speaks of the land being overrun, oppressed and impoverished.

In the passage we are considering it is important to note that the judgement of locusts follows the judgement of drought. It is the next step in judgement if you will. The drought affects the ability of the earth to produce, then come the locusts to take the little which it does produce. These judgements of the Lord are progressive in nature. The locusts follow the drought and increase the effect of the Lord's judgements upon mankind.

3.   Pestilence

If I send pestilence among my people (2Ch 7:13)

The third judgement of the Lord. The Lord <u>shuts</u> the heavens, He <u>commands</u> the locusts and now He <u>sends</u> pestilence. The Lord <u>acts</u>, the Lord <u>commands</u> and now the Lord <u>sends</u>.

The Hebrew word for pestilence as used here means "in the sense of destroying" and is translated murrain, pestilence, plague. The word is used throughout scripture and has an unmistakable link to death.

    a)   In Exodus 9 this same Hebrew word is used for the fifth plague that the Lord unleashed against the nation. This plague was to be upon all of the livestock of Egypt. There the Lord pronounced that any livestock left in the field would die. Egypt suffered great losses here and we are told in verse 6 that all the cattle of Egypt died.

    b)   In Leviticus 26:25 the Lord declares that Israel would suffer pestilence and then be given into the hands of their enemies if they continued in a life of disobedience.

    c)   In 2 Samuel 24:13 pestilence is seen as a judgement of death upon the people for sin. Here again the Lord lists three judgements, pestilence being the third. Pestilence here saw seventy thousand men perish.

Pestilence is unmistakeably linked with death in the scriptures and is seen here as the final judgement of the Lord. This is the end result of a shut heaven and locusts being sent. This judgement naturally follows the first two and is the fulness of them.

Throughout these three judgements of the Lord we see the progressive nature of the judgements. With each new judgement we see an escalation in the effects. Drought makes life hard, locusts attack hope and pestilence takes life. As God tries again and again to gain the attention of man, the judgements increase until man takes notice. It is the same thing that we see with the judgement against Pharaoh in Exodus. The judgements increased until Pharaoh finally softened his heart before the Lord. It should be noted that these judgements of the Lord are designed to bring the people of the Lord back to Him. They are designed to soften our hearts and cause us to understand that the Lord is trying to get our attention. He forewarns us of His judgements so that when we see them we may quickly recognise them and return to Him.

C. The People
If my people, which are called by my name, shall humble themselves, and pray, and seek my face, and turn from their wicked ways; then will I hear from heaven, and will forgive their sin, and will heal their land. (2Ch 7:14)

In this next verse we are presented with an "If" Statement by the Lord. An "If" statement is a statement that declares "If" certain conditions are met "Then" there will be a predetermined response. We see here that it is the Lord who sets the conditions and then outlines what the predetermined response will be.

An extension to the "If" statement, is the "If, Then, Else". This follows the pattern as outlined above but goes further to outline the predetermined response if the conditions are not met, i.e. "Else". In the passage under consideration the "Else" in this case is implied. The Lord says that "If" His people will return, "Then" He will answer. The implied "Else" is that if His people won't respond, then He won't answer i.e. "If" His people will return "Then" He will answer, "Else" He won't.

If we were to amend the above passage to an "If, Then, Else" statement it would read.

IF: (conditions to be met)
1. My people who are called by My name
2. Will humble themselves
3. And pray
4. And seek My face
5. And turn from their wicked ways

THEN: (The predetermined response if the conditions are met)
1. He will hear from heaven

Exposition

2. He will forgive their sin
3. He will heal their land

ELSE (The response if the conditions aren't met)
1. He will not hear
2. He will not forgive
3. He will not heal

Our focus in this section will be on those conditions that make up the "If" part of the above statement. As we look at this verse broken down we can see that there are five conditions that the Lord outlines as part of the "If" statement which we will consider here. We will consider the "Then" and the "Else" in the next sections of this study. As we move into this "If" section of verse 14 we start by considering just who the Lord is referring to when He says my people.

1. If My people who are called by My name
If My people, which are called by My name… (2Ch 7:14)

This is the first condition of the "If" statement. It is worth noting that the Lord puts a double emphasis on who He is talking to here. So often when we read or think about the judgements of the Lord we associate the need to repent, seek the Lord etc with those who have transgressed. But that is not what the Lord is saying here. He is very clearing stating that He is addressing His people who are called by His name. He is very clearly talking to, in this case, those people of Israel who followed Him. The onus of responsibility here is placed upon the faithful believers. If MY people who are called by MY name. This language is inapplicable to those who have walked away, it is directed to those who are in covenantal relationship with the Lord.

This is possibly the most important point that we need to understand about this "If" statement. Before we look at the other conditions and what is required in response to the judgement of the Lord it is vital that we understand that He is addressing those people who are in relationship with Him. Not those who were, or those that might be but those who are. The conditions that come next are directed to the Lord's people. The Lord starts by qualifying who He is talking to and then goes on to list the conditions required of them when His judgements are in effect.

As we move forward through the other four parts of the "If" statement we need to constantly keep in mind that the message of the Lord conveyed here is to His people called by His name.

2. Shall humble themselves
…shall humble themselves…(2Ch 7:14)

The Hebrew word for humble as used here is 'kana' and means: to bend the knee; to humiliate, vanquish. It is used some forty-three times in the Old Testament and carries the thought of willingly bowing oneself down and coming under the subjection of a greater power, be it in the natural or spiritual.

In this particular instance it is referring to a complete recognition of God as the sovereign Lord and bowing down before Him in complete subjugation in understanding of who He is. When we humble ourselves before the Lord every facet of religious pride is dropped. We do not care about how things appear, we do not care about what people think, we do not care who is watching, our sole focus is humbly coming before the Lord. We bow before Him who is greater. It is important to note that humility is not just an action, but it is an attitude of heart that we show forth. This will become more evident as we move forward.

Let us consider some examples of humility from the Word:

a) Moses

In Numbers 12:3 Moses is described as the humblest (meekest) man upon the earth in his generation. Moses is a fascinating character study in himself but in the writer's mind the verse that best illustrates this truth is found in Exodus 33:15. Shortly after the golden calf incident, Moses is speaking with the Lord and as the conversation progresses Moses pleads with the Lord for His presence to go with them on the journey:

And he said unto him, If thy presence go not with me, carry us not up hence.(Exo 33:15)

Moses, by this time, was a great leader. He oversaw and shepherded the people. He knew how to lead, yet he knew that without the help of the Lord any attempt at progressing was in vain. Moses understood his complete need for the help of the Lord in leading the people of Israel. If Moses had been proud he would have looked to his own abilities to achieve things, as he once had (Acts 7:24-25). But Moses was humble and understood his great need of the Lord. That is the essence of humility as in the case we are looking at. It is an understanding that no matter how great our own strengths and abilities are, if we have not the Lord, we cannot accomplish that which He has called us to. It is the Lord who is our great helper and our need resides in Him.

b) The Prodigal Son

In Luke 15:12-32 we read of the account of the prodigal son. The prodigal son lived a life of blessing and sought his inheritance early so that he could go out and enjoy the pleasures of life. For a while things went well and he was living the highlife, surrounded by friends. He soon ran out of money though, at a time when the land was entering great famine. The prodigal son found himself in a time of judgement. He had stepped away from His father and chosen his own path. He had gone from the blessing of his father, to living the high life surrounded by friends, to being alone, feeding pigs and longing to fill his mouth with the food of swine. Such was his fall.

At this low point he had the realisation that he needed to return to his father. He did not return in pride and entitlement though, expecting to walk back into his father's arms as if nothing had happened. He returned in true humility. He prepared himself to return under his father's covering not as a son, but as a servant. In his low estate the pride of the prodigal had been dealt with and he returned in humility and repentance appealing for the mercy of his father.

c)   The Tax Collector

In Luke 18:9-14 we read of the pharisee and the tax collector. The pharisee came before the Lord in pride, exalting himself above others and gloating about his good works. The tax collector came before the Lord but would only stand at a distance. He wouldn't lift his eyes to heaven but beat his breast and plead for the mercy of the Lord. The tax collector understood who he was and he understood who God was. For his approach Jesus commends him as an example of humility. In true humility of spirit, the tax collector came before the Lord. His approach was all about God and unlike the pharisee was absolutely nothing about himself.

True humility is a reflection of attitude and something that cannot be faked. It is an internal attitude that also reveals itself with outward actions. The actual act of bowing in humility is in response to one's attitude of heart. It is to admit our deep need for God's help in our lives and the situations that lay before us. It is a recognition that we are not the answer to the problem and the only solution is the intervention of the Lord. Moses, the prodigal and the tax collector all had this insight. Their actions of humility flowed from the attitude that was in their hearts.

When the Lord says if My people shall humble themselves, He is not saying that they need come before Him in humility as a once off action. Humility is an attitude that develops and is an act that repeats. The Lord is saying that there is a way in which the people of God need to live. The call of the Lord here is for His people to return to a life of humility before Him. If My people will live in the knowledge of who I am, with an understanding of their need for My help and demonstrate this through how they live, then I will hear.

It is important to note that the need for the people of God to humble themselves is the first thing that the Lord lists in this passage. It is the first step and key to all that follows.

To summarise, humility in the verse under investigation, is not only the recognition of a greater power, but coming under His authority and seeking His help and intervention. It is an attitude of heart, revealed in action that shows our reverence for Him who is greater.

3. And Pray
...and pray...(2Ch 7:14)

The Hebrew word for pray as used here is 'palal'. It is used some eighty-four times in the Bible and carries with it the thought of intercession. Prayer with intercession involves not only seeking the Lord but also standing in the gap with and for someone or something. It is the type of prayer that implies both effort and persistence. This is not just presenting a list of requests to the Lord, but involves prayer with a deep urgency and passion. This is the kind of prayer that is referred to in James Chapter 5.

.... The effectual fervent prayer of a righteous man availeth much. (Jas 5:16)

Fervency in prayer is an inner fire that can only be released through allowing prayer to flow out of us. It is recognising and understanding the need before us and knowing that the only possible intervention is if the Lord is to step in. Our fervency and intercession is directed at the Lord to intervene.

A great example of this is seen with Abraham interceding for Lot in Genesis 18. As the Lord pronounced His judgement on the city of Sodom, Abraham recognised that he needed to stand in the gap for Lot and intercede in prayer before the Lord for him. Years earlier Abraham and Lot had parted ways as the land could not sustain both of their herds and flocks, such were their number. Lot chose a path that led him down to Sodom and it was here he eventually settled with his family. As the judgement of the Lord sounds in the ears of Abraham his heart was immediately stirred for his nephew who would be affected by what was going to happen.

In this account Abraham goes back to the Lord six times in an effort to intercede for his nephew. Six times Abraham returns to the Lord and intercedes for the life of his nephew and his family. Abraham stood in the gap for Lot seeking the Lord's mercy on his behalf. Abraham recognised the urgency of the situation and continued in prayer unto the Lord. He was fervent and persistent and the Lord heard him because of this.

The call in this passage from 2 Chronicles is for the people of God to pray fervently. This call is not to an individual, but to the people of the Lord collectively. The call is to My people (plural) called by My name. So in as much as there is individual application there is also corporate application. It is a broad call that covers praying at home, praying in small groups and praying at Church. The Lord is looking for a people who are humble enough to persist in prayer until they receive an answer. We see this in Luke 18 where the call of Jesus is for us to be like the persistent widow who continually came before

Exposition

the unjust judge seeking justice (See Luke 18:1-8). She never gave up. She persisted in coming before the judge and presenting her plea.

The prayers that are referred to in 2 Chronicles 7:14 are no doubt related to the judgements of the Lord as listed in verse 13. It is these situations that should prompt us to acknowledge our need of the Lord's help. When we humble ourselves and recognise that absolute need for the Lord's intervention in a situation then prayer should be the natural resulting action. After the people of the Lord have returned in humility to the Lord they are to pray.

1) If My people
2) Shall humble themselves
3) And pray

Returning in humility comes first and is followed by prayer. It is not if My people shall pray and humble themselves, it is if My people will first of all humble themselves and then pray. God opposes the proud but gives grace to the humble (James 4:6). The ears of the Lord are open to the humble prayers of His saints.

> *The LORD is far from the wicked: but he heareth the prayer of the righteous. (Pro 15:29)*

The promise of the Lord is that He will hear our prayers. The question though is whether the people of God will humble themselves and pray? Are we presenting prayers for Him to hear? The responsibility lies with us.

4. And seek My face
…and seek My face… (2Ch 7:14)

To seek the face of someone is to put our effort into meeting with them and be in their presence. When we truly want to meet with someone we adjust our schedules and lives to try and make the meeting happen.

To seek the face of the Lord is to wholeheartedly pursue Him with all that we have. It is to put Him first and foremost in our lives on a continual basis. It is to go after Him with all that we have. To seek the face of God is to fit our activities around Him rather than squeezing Him in around our activities. It requires us to realign our lives. It is to make Him the priority and not an optional extra. Seeking the face of the Lord is to pursue Him with a passion that can only be quenched by His presence, for to seek His face is to seek to be in His presence.

In Daniel 9, Daniel was prompted to seek the Lord after receiving revelation from studying the book of Jeremiah and gaining an understanding that the time of Judah's captivity by Babylon would soon be coming to an end. In verse three we are told:

> *And I set my face unto the Lord God, to seek by prayer and supplications, with fasting, and sackcloth, and ashes: (Dan 9:3)*

The priority for Daniel was the Lord and this is the essence of what it means to seek the face of the Lord. The things of this world became less important to Daniel as he focused on seeking the Lord. His food, his clothes and his appearance took second place to his pursuit of seeking after the Father. Daniel's face was set to seek the face of the Lord. His gaze was transfixed and his purpose was set. The other things of life had to be accommodated around this priority.

To seek the face of the Lord is to go after Him with all we have and all that we are. The things of life become less important as our focus to be in His presence becomes paramount in our lives. He is our priority and focus. Seeking His face is to be something that we should continually do as believers.

> *Seek the LORD, and his strength: seek his face evermore. (Psa 105:4)*

It is an attitude of life the Lord is wanting His people to have. The Word tells us that Jesus stands at the door and knocks (Rev 3:20). He has already set His focus on seeking each of us, He is just waiting for us to respond in kind.

5. And turn from their wicked ways
… and turn from their wicked ways (2Ch 7:14)

We need to remember that here the Lord is talking to His people, called by His name. This is a message to God's people.

To turn from is to change one's stance. It is to make a one hundred and eighty degree change in direction. We turn from one thing and change our gaze to face another. To turn from a wicked way, is to turn from going towards it and point ourselves in another direction.

So what exactly is a wicked way? A wicked way is really anything that is opposite to the commands of God. These are not necessarily massive errors in the lives of His people (though they can be), but can be any path, however minor, that isn't leading towards Him.

Exposition

This statement is a reminder that whilst we are all being perfected none of us are yet perfect and at times we need to realign our steps to make sure that we haven't strayed from the narrow path (Mar 7:14).

1 Peter 4:17 tells us that the time is come that judgement must start with the House of God and Jesus Himself tells us that we must consider the log in our own eyes before judging the speck in others (Mat 4:4).

In the writer's mind though, whilst this call to turn incorporates personal repentance as discussed above, it also goes beyond that. It also involves a corporate aspect. In our previous point we looked at the example of Daniel in Daniel Chapter 9:3 where Daniel sought the face of the Lord. In Daniel 9:4-19 we see that immediately after Daniel makes this decision to seek the face of the Lord, he seeks the Lord in prayer and intercession. We see here that Daniel pours out his petition before the Lord in intercession not just for himself but for the nation. He acknowledges the sins of the nation and how they had turned their backs on the commands of God and had not listened to the prophets. He lays it all out before the Lord and seeks His mercy and forgiveness.

Daniel goes beyond humbling himself, praying, seeking the Lord's face and turning from his wicked ways from an individual point of view. He expands his petition to the include the whole nation and intercedes as one of them. Daniel was a righteous man yet throughout his prayer the language he uses is constantly collective. That is, it is never I or they, but rather the collective we. Daniel identifies himself as part of the nation that had turned from God. He takes ownership and accountability for it and stands in the gap with and on behalf of his nation. Daniel is interceding in prayer on behalf of the people for the forgiveness of their sins.

The reader is encouraged to read and meditate on this passage of scripture and see the heart that Daniel had.

As we have looked at the first part of 2 Chronicles 7:14 we discovered the "If" statement presented by the Lord to His people. Throughout the five conditions of this "If" statement we see that the onus of responsibilities for these conditions being met lies solely with the people of God. This is not a call to unbelievers but to believers, those that would call themselves children of God. It is "If" the children of God will humble themselves, and pray, and seek His face and turn from their wicked ways. It is "If" His people will fulfil all of these conditions. It is not a people, but His people. It is not one condition or two conditions, but all of the five conditions of the "If" statement. That is the truth that the Lord is laying out. If you want the "Then" you must fulfil all of the "If". The Lord will do His part, but it is contingent upon the people of God fulfilling theirs. If the people of God can do that, they then experience the "Then". "If" My people who are called by My name, will humble themselves, and pray, and seek My face and turn from their wicked ways "Then".

D. The Response
....THEN will I hear from heaven, and will forgive their sin, and will heal their land. (2Ch 7:14)

If the conditions that the Lord outlines are met, then the people of the Lord will get to experience the response of the Lord or the "Then" part of the "If" statement.

The Lord says here that "If" the people of God fulfil their part then He will hear their prayer, He will forgive their sins and He will heal their land. Notice the three I wills of God here. I will hear. I will forgive. I will heal. These three I wills of God are focused on the restoration of man. For the reader compare these to the five I wills of Satan which are focused on self in Isa 14:13-14.

These three statements of the Lord are really three promises. The Lord is declaring what His responses will be when His people return unto Him with a passion to seek His face.

1. I will hear
THEN will I hear from heaven (2Ch 7:14)

The first promise of the Lord. I will hear. Not I might hear or I will possibly hear, but a definitive I will hear. What a comfort to know that the Lord will hear the cries of His people. Our prayers do not fall on deaf ears.

> *The eyes of the LORD are upon the righteous,* ***and His ears are open unto their cry.*** *(Psa 34:15)*
>
> *Now we know that God heareth not sinners:* ***but if any man be a worshipper of God, and doeth his will, him He heareth.*** *(Joh 9:31)*
>
> *The LORD is far from the wicked: but* ***He heareth the prayer of the righteous.*** *(Pro 15:29)*
>
> *I cried unto God with my voice, even unto God with my voice;* ***and He gave ear unto me.*** *(Psa 77:1)*

We have a security in the fact that the Lord hears the prayers of His people. Over and over in scripture He tells us that His ears are attentive to the prayers of the righteous. The issue is never whether the Lord is listening to His people, it is whether His people are calling unto Him. The Lord waits with an attentive ear to hear the prayers of His saints.

2. I will forgive
and will forgive their sin (2Ch 7:14)

Exposition

The second promise of the Lord. He will forgive. The Lord is ready, willing and able to forgive the sins of man. There is no doubt that this has reference to His people repenting from their wicked ways and interceding for their nation after the example of Daniel.

The Lord forgives and removes the stain of sin.

> *Come now, and let us reason together, saith the LORD: though your sins be as scarlet, they shall be as white as snow; though they be red like crimson, they shall be as wool. (Isa 1:18)*

> *As far as the east is from the west, so far hath he removed our transgressions from us. (Psa 103:12)*

If we turn and repent unto Him, He will forgive our sin. That is His promise unto us.

3. I will heal
and will heal their land. (2Ch 7:14)

The third promise of the Lord. I will heal. It is another definitive declaration.

Scripture declares the Lord to be Jehovah Rapha, the Lord who heals. In response to His people the Lord brings healing. He heals the drought by restoring rain. He heals the land by restoring what the locust has eaten. He heals pestilence from His people and supplies life. He heals completely, fully and unconditionally.

The Lord's promise is to heal. The land is healed from the judgements that have been inflicted upon it. This healing occurs through the provision of blessings that stand in contrast to the judgements of the Lord. The law of opposites applies here. A shut heaven is replaced with rain. That which the locusts have eaten is replaced with harvest and provision. Pestilence is replaced with life. In healing the Lord turns the people away from judgement and into blessing.

Judgements	Healing/Blessing
Drought	Rain
Locusts devouring	Harvest
Pestilence	Life

The healing of the Lord is the direct opposite of His judgements. The two stand diametrically opposed. When the Lord heals, we receive the opposite of judgement, we receive blessing.

The Lord has declared that He will respond to His people, BUT: Prayer has to be offered to be heard; Sin has to be repented of to be forgiven; His people must return if He is to heal. The Lord cannot hear that which isn't spoken. He can't forgive that which isn't repented of. He won't heal if His people don't return. The onus lies with His people. The Lord unequivocally will respond in every way that He has promised "If" His people will return unto Him. "If" His people fulfil the conditions laid out for them, "Then" the Lord responds, "Else" He doesn't. This is the implied "Else" of the "If" statement. If the conditions outlined by the Lord aren't met then He won't respond. This is the Else.

IF	THEN	ELSE
My people who are called by My name	I will hear	I won't hear
Shall humble themselves	I will forgive	I won't forgive
And pray	I will heal	I won't heal
And seek My face		
And turn from their wicked ways		

The Lord's response (the "Then") is readily available so long as His people fulfil the "If" conditions. "If" His people return, "Then" He responds, "Else" He doesn't.

E. <u>The Promise</u>
Now mine eyes shall be open, and mine ears attent unto the prayer that is made in this place. (2Ch 7:15)

The Lord's focus is on His chosen place. Solomon's prayer was that the Lord would ever be attentive to prayer made at the Temple. The Lord responds and says He is watching and listening always. His focus is always upon the chosen place and He waits attentively for His people. That is the great promise. He waits for us. He waits for His people to respond at the chosen place. His eyes are ever fixed and His ears are ever open to that which is offered in His chosen place.

Exposition Summary

If My People

EXPOSITION SUMMARY

In our Exposition we broke down the Word of the Lord to Solomon in 2 Chronicles 7:11-16. In doing this we discovered five main points:

A. <u>The Chosen Place</u>
The chosen place of the Lord referred to in this passage of scripture is the Temple of Solomon. The Lord showed His acceptance and His choice of the temple when His Holy fire of the Lord fell on the day of dedication. It is the Holy accepting fire of the Lord that shows His choice. His fire declares His chosen place.

Connected and intertwined with the chosen place are prayer and sacrifice. The three are distinct yet related. The Lord declares that His chosen place is a place of heard prayer and sacrifice.

B. <u>The Judgements</u>
The Lord outlines three judgements that would fall:

1. There would be no rain. The heavens are shut, there is no provision of water to man which leads to reduced provision of crops and harvest. Life affected.
2. Locusts – lack of provision, oppression and impoverishment. A nation being overrun. The little that is left from the drought is taken. Hope affected.
3. Pestilence – Death, the opposite of life and the end result of the first two judgements. Life taken.

These three judgements are progressive and each is intended to try and capture the attention of His people and cause them to turn back to Him.

C. <u>The People</u>
In this section we saw that there were five conditions laid upon the people. These conditions formed the "If" part of our "If" statement. The five conditions the Lord outlines are "If":

1. My people who are called by My name - The people referred to here are the people of the Lord. His children. Those that are called by His name It is not unbelievers or heathen nations, but those that belong to the Lord.
2. Shall humble themselves - True humility, flowing from the heart in recognition of who God is.
3. And pray – Passionate intercessory prayer where we stand in the gap with and for those we are praying for.
4. And seek My face – Prioritising the pursuit of His presence.

5. And turn from their wicked ways – repenting and turning away from anything that doesn't exalt or lead to the Lord.

Upon His people the Lord lays five conditions and "If" His people will respond to them, "Then" He will come in mercy. It is up to His people to respond in the ways the Lord has outlined if they want to see Him bring blessing and heal the condition of their land as outlined in vs 13.

D. The Response

The Lord outlines three things that He will do. The response of the Lord here forms the "Then" part of our "If" statement. "If" His people will return unto Him "Then":

1. He will hear – He hears the cry of His people.
2. He will forgive – as His people turn from their wicked ways.
3. He will heal – He heals the land by sending rain, bringing harvest and restoring life. His judgements are healed by His blessings.

The Lord is ever faithful, but His response is determined by the actions of His people.

E. The Promise

The Lord's eyes are ever upon and His ears are ever attentive to His chosen place. His people are to respond to Him at His chosen place. He is waiting there for them.

As we move forward in our study we will carry through the points we discovered in this section to our next sections on Example and Application. As we do this we will hopefully see the flow of truth as revealed through the Word.

EXAMPLE

Seeing the truths of 2 Chronicles 7 confirmed through scriptural example.

In meditating on the exposition part of this study the Lord impressed upon the writer the need for not only the people of God to stand, but also the need for them to stand in the gap. It was on this thought that the Lord led the writer to another passage of scripture which demonstrates what we have been talking about so far. Whenever the Lord communicates truth, He never does it once. His truth is witnessed and attested to through its occurrences in scripture.

The Lord sets forth that in the mouth of two or three witnesses every matter is established. This is a law that God himself abides by. In our first section we looked at the witness of truth in Exposition, here we look at the same witness of truth in Example.

We see this example of truth in 1 Kings 18 where we read of the account of Elijah and the prophets of Baal. In 1 Kings 17 Elijah declares a drought upon the land according to the Word of the Lord. After three and a half years Elijah emerges from hiding and presents himself before wicked King Ahab. Elijah instructs King Ahab to gather together all the prophets of Baal and all of the prophets of the grove that ate at Jezebels table and to meet him upon Mount Carmel with all of the people of Israel. Once all were gathered together upon the mount, Elijah set a mandate that today Israel had to decide who was their God, they could no longer sway between two opinions. They would have to choose between Baal and the Lord. In order to do this Elijah set a challenge between himself and the prophets of Baal. Both would offer the same sacrifice unto their God and the God who answered by fire would be Lord. The prophets of Baal agreed to this challenge and for almost a whole day they did everything that was in their custom to seek an answer from their god, but none came. At the time of the evening sacrifice Elijah assumes his turn to seek his God. He prepares the evening sacrifice and instructs that a trench be dug around the altar and asks three distinct times that water be poured over the sacrifice and the wooden altar until the trench was full. As Elijah sought the Lord, the fire of God descended from heaven and consumed the sacrifice, the altar and licked up all of the water in the trench. Upon seeing this demonstration from the Lord the people of Israel fell on their faces, they returned to the Lord and the prophets of Baal were struck down. Elijah then sought the Lord for the drought to end. He bowed himself down before the Lord seven times, each time asking his servant to check the horizon. After his seventh time of interceding a small cloud appeared on the horizon. The sky was soon black with clouds and there was a great outpouring on the land. The reader is encouraged to read all of 1 Kings 18 before moving forward with this section.

Example

It was in meditating upon this passage of scripture that the Lord spoke to the writer the same truths as that of 2 Chronicles 7:11-16. As we move through this section it is the writers hope that the reader too sees the unfolding of this truth and how this passage is a clear example of the truths we discovered in our exposition on 2 Chronicles 7.

A. <u>The Chosen Place</u>
Unlike 2 Chronicles 7 the chosen place is not directly mentioned here in 1 Kings 18. However, as we consider the revelation of scripture here this truth soon becomes apparent. As we move through this passage from 1 Kings, we will also see again the connection of the chosen place, prayer and sacrifice as we did in Chronicles.

1. The Place

In 1 Kings 18 we read of the stand that Elijah took against the prophets of Baal. After the Lord proved himself here and the people returned unto Him, Elijah and the people of Israel took the prophets of Baal down to the brook Kishon and slew them there. Just after this Elijah tells King Ahab to get up and drink for there was the sound of the abundance of rain. Elijah declared this in faith and would then go and pray to the Lord for the rain. What caught the writer's attention was Elijah's actions after making this announcement.

> ………… *And Elijah went up to the top of Carmel; and he cast himself down upon the earth, and put his face between his knees, (1Ki 18:42)*

Elijah had just been on top of Mount Carmel where he had his challenge with the Prophets of Baal. He then came down to the brook Kishon with the people of Israel where the prophets of Baal were slain. Elijah then heads back up the mountain once again. Why was he now going back up the mountain? Why could he have not stayed at the brook and prayed there? Why did he return up the mountain and there cast himself down before the Lord?

To understand this, we need to look at what happened when Elijah presented his offering before the Lord in the presence of Israel. We pick this up in verse 30 of 1 Kings 18 and there are several points for us to note as we consider what happened here.

a) The Mountain
So Ahab sent unto all the children of Israel, and gathered the prophets together unto mount Carmel. (1Ki 18:20)

Elijah and the people of Israel were gathered on Mount Carmel. This was not a temple or a building, but a mountain in Israel.

b) The Rebuilt Altar

After the prophets of Baal had tried all day to summon their god without success, Elijah stepped in and announced that it was his turn. He starts by rebuilding or repairing the altar of the Lord that was broken down. Scripture doesn't record when this altar was erected but from this passage it is evident that:

1) An altar had been built here.
2) It was an altar unto the Lord.
3) It has been neglected and allowed to fall into disrepair.

In commenting on this particular passage Matthew Henry puts forth: "He fitted up an altar. He would not make use of theirs, which had been polluted with their prayers to Baal, but, finding the ruins of an altar there, which had formerly been used in the service of the Lord, he chose to repair that (1Kings 18:30), to intimate to them that he was not about to introduce any new religion, but to revive the faith and worship of their fathers' God, and reduce them to their first love, their first works."[1]

In repairing the altar of the Lord Elijah took twelve stones, one for each of the tribes of Israel and built the altar from these.

c) The Time

*And it came to pass **at the time of the offering of the evening sacrifice**, that Elijah the prophet came near, and said, LORD God of Abraham, Isaac, and of Israel, let it be known this day that thou art God in Israel, and that I am thy servant, and that I have done all these things at thy word. (1Ki 18:36)*

Elijah waited all day, until the time of the evening sacrifice. He had rebuilt the altar and upon it he offered a bull for sacrifice. Elijah was functioning in the role of a priest here, interceding for the nation. He offered a burnt offering unto the Lord in accordance with Leviticus 1:6-8. Elijah was offering a prescribed sacrifice, in the prescribed way at a prescribed time in obedience to the Word of the Lord.

d) The Fire

Elijah had prepared the altar, he had dug a trench around it and he had laid the sacrifice upon it. Before he prays though he asks the people to fill four barrels with water and to pour them out upon the altar. He had them repeat this three times, so a total of twelve barrels of water were poured out. The sacrifice was wet, the wood soaked and the trench full. Elijah then sought the Lord in prayer and said:

LORD God of Abraham, Isaac, and of Israel, let it be known this day that thou art God in Israel, and that I am thy servant, and that I have done all these things at

---

[1] Matthew Henry's commentary on the Whole Bible, 1 Kings 18:21-40.

thy word. Hear me, O LORD, hear me, that this people may know that thou art the LORD God, and that thou hast turned their heart back again. (1Ki 18:36-37)

The Lord heard the prayer of Elijah and responded to it in the presence of the people. It is here that we again see the fire of the Lord fall:

Then the fire of the LORD fell, and consumed the burnt sacrifice, and the wood, and the stones, and the dust, and licked up the water that was in the trench. (1Ki 18:38)

The divine fire of the Lord fell once again. The fire of the Lord fell and it consumed the offering, the wood the burnt offering was offered on, the stones of the altar, the dust around it and all of the twelve barrels of water that had been poured out. What a sight this must have been. How awesome this must have been to witness.

It is this fire of the Lord the answers the question we posed at the start of this point. The reason Elijah climbed back up Mount Carmel after descending to the brook Kishon, was because the Lord had shown Mount Carmel to be His chosen place through the outpouring of His divine fire. Mount Carmel was the place where the fire of God fell, just like it had done in the Temple of Solomon. It is to be remembered that the Temple of Solomon was still standing in the country of Judah, but Elijah wasn't compelled by the Lord to go there and pray. Instead the fire of the Lord fell on Mount Carmel in the land of Israel highlighting to Elijah where he was to pray.

Just as the Lord had signified His acceptance and choice of the Temple of Solomon as the chosen place through the pouring out of His divine fire in acceptance so here He demonstrates the same truth on Mount Carmel. The fire of the Lord not only showed that the Lord had chosen Mount Carmel but also set Mount Carmel apart as holy unto the Lord. This is the truth set forth and a truth that Elijah obviously understood. It was because of this that Elijah returned to the top of Mount Carmel to pray. The Lord had shown that Mount Carmel was His chosen place where prayer was to be offered.

2. The Place of Heard Prayer
Hear me, O LORD, hear me, that this people may know that thou art the LORD God, and that thou hast turned their heart back again. (1Ki 18:37)

It was at the chosen place that the Lord answered the prayer of Elijah and revealed Himself to the nation of Israel as the one true God. The two are shown to be particularly interconnected in this example. We see from 1 Kings that the Lord immediately rained down His Holy anointing fire in answer to Elijah's prayer. Elijah was heard at the place chosen by the Lord. This would shortly be further confirmed to Elijah when he interceded for the drought to end.

3. The Place of Sacrifice

*And it came to pass at the time of the **offering of the evening sacrifice**, that Elijah the prophet came near, and said, LORD God of Abraham, Isaac, and of Israel, let it be known this day that thou art God in Israel, and that I am thy servant, and that I have done all these things at thy word. (1Ki 18:36)*

The Chosen place was a place of sacrifice. As we have touched on above, the sacrifice was done according to the specifications of the Lord at the designated time. The sacrifice was according to Gods standards and it was offered at the chosen place. Elijah operated in the role of the prophet/priest here offering the sacrifice for the nation of Israel.

In the three verses of 1 Kings 18:37 – 39 we see sacrifice, prayer (that was offered and heard) and the evidence of the chosen place. Just as we saw with the Temple for Solomon these three things are interwoven and connected. The chosen place is a place of prayer and a place of sacrifice.

2 Chronicles 7	1 Kings 18
Temple of Solomon	Mount Carmel
Solomon	Elijah
Fire of the Lord fell	Fire of the Lord fell
Divine Acceptance	Divine Acceptance
Divine Choice	Divine Choice
Place where prayer would be heard	Place where prayer was heard
Place of Sacrifice	Place where sacrifice was offered
The Chosen Place	The Chosen Place

B. The Judgements

As we move into this section, we will see that the judgements mentioned in 2 Chronicles 7 align to the situation in Israel at the time we are considering in 1 Kings.

1. Drought

In 1 Kings 17:1 we see the judgement of the Lord announced through Elijah to King Ahab:

And Elijah the Tishbite, who was of the inhabitants of Gilead, said unto Ahab, As the LORD God of Israel liveth, before whom I stand, there shall not be dew nor rain these years, but according to my word. (1Ki 17:1)

The judgement of the Lord against the nation of Israel was that of drought. There would be no rain and there would be no dew. No moisture to nourish the land at all. This would continue until the Word of the Lord came through the prophet Elijah. The heavens were shut in judgement according to the Word of the Lord. For three and a half years the nation of Israel received no rain.

2. Locusts Devouring

Whilst the judgement of the Lord started as a drought in 1 Kings 17, in 1 Kings 18 we see the flow on effects and further judgements of the Lord evidenced. We read there that after several years of drought king Ahab calls the governor of his house, Obadiah, and outlines that he and Obadiah were to go throughout the land looking for feed for the livestock.

> *And Ahab said unto Obadiah, Go into the land, unto all fountains of water, and unto all brooks: peradventure we may find grass to save the horses and mules alive, that we lose not all the beasts. (1Ki 18:5)*

What had started as a drought now meant that there was no feed for the livestock in the land. This thought is confirmed by 1 Kings 18:2 where it says that there was a famine in the land. The land could not produce enough to fully sustain life. Part of the judgement of a shut heaven is a lack of crops and harvest. Harvest is diminished when there is no rain. But the situation here goes beyond that and moves into the area of a nation being impoverished. We read here that there was scarcity of any provision within the land. This aligns with the thought of the locusts devouring the land. The locusts eliminate provision, they oppress a nation and impoverish it completely. The little that is produced from a lack of rain is destroyed. There had been drought, the judgement of no rain and now there was famine and impoverishment, the judgement of locusts.

3. Pestilence

At this point in time the nation of Israel had no provision and Ahab and Obadiah were on a mission to try and find some. The reason given for this mission is to find feed for the horses and mules so that that they would not lose all the beasts. Whilst they were trying to save some, the clear indication is that they had lost some beasts already and would lose more if they weren't successful in their task. To lose a beast is to have them die. This relates to the pestilence judgement of 2 Chronicles 7:14. The very fact the they are looking for grass to save the horses and mules so that they don't lose all the beasts would imply that other livestock, such as sheep and goats, may have already started to pass. The judgement of pestilence was already prevalent in the land.

So we see here, in the time of Elijah, the exact judgements referred to in 2 Chronicles 7:

2 Chronicles 7	1 Kings 18
Heaven shut, no rain	No rain or dew for three and a half years, harvest affected
Locusts to devour the land	No grass or provision for the livestock. Famine, impoverishment of a nation
Pestilence	Death of livestock

Israel was living through and experiencing the same judgements of the Lord as were outlined to Solomon. In 1 Kings 18 we see the judgements of the Lord in action against the nation of Israel. We also see here again the progressive nature of the judgements of the Lord. Drought leads to famine and impoverishment which leads to death. The judgements progress and escalate until His people return unto Him. His judgements were indeed taking place in the land.

C. <u>The People</u>
As we look at this point, we will again see the same truths that were illustrated in 2 Chronicles. We see the same five "If" requirements laid out and further to this we see that once they have been met, the Lord responds with His "Then".

1. My People who are called by My Name

The onus here was upon Elijah and the nation of Israel. It was unto the people of Abraham, Isaac and Jacob, the chosen nation of the Lord that the responsibility rests upon here. His people were to return unto Him. This was the challenge that Elijah set forth, and this is indeed what happened. It wasn't a call to a foreign nation, or to the worshippers of Baal but unto the people of Israel, the Lord's people.

2. Shall humble themselves

In our Exposition section we noted that to humble oneself was to have a complete recognition of God as the one true God and bowing down before Him in complete understanding of who He is. It is an attitude of heart based in reverence and respect for who God is.

In Chapter 18 of 1 Kings we see both God's people and Elijah humble themselves before the Lord.

a) The people of the Lord

In verse 18 we read that after the Lord pours out His Holy fire in the presence of the congregation, that the people fell on their faces and declared that the Lord is God.

And when all the people saw it, they fell on their faces: and they said, The LORD, he is the God; the LORD, he is the God. (1Ki 18:39)

As the fire of the Lord fell from Heaven so the people fell to the earth. They no longer stood in pride waiting for the Lord to prove himself, they lay prostrate in recognition of who God was. They no longer stood in arrogance challenging God to prove himself, they lay with their faces to the ground in humility before the presence of the Lord. The fell on their faces and declared, The Lord He is God. They humbled themselves.

Example

b)   Elijah

When Elijah ascended the Mount to pray we are told that Elijah similarly humbled himself before the Lord.

> *So Ahab went up to eat and to drink. And Elijah went up to the top of Carmel; and he cast himself down upon the earth, and put his face between his knees, (1Ki 18:42)*

Elijah ascended the Mount and cast himself down to the ground in the chosen place of the Lord. He fell to the ground, with his face between his knees. Elijah humbles himself before the Lord before seeking Him in prayer. In true humility Elijah seeks for the Lords intervention with the judgements that were upon the land.

3.   And pray

Elijah is the individual who prays in this instance. We see with Elijah the persistent nature of prayer needed when the people of the Lord seek Him for the judgement He has poured out to end.

We are told that upon humbling himself Elijah sought the Lord in prayer. He sought the Lord for the heavens to open and rain to come forth. He interceded for the nation that the drought would end. After bowing himself down in prayer and intercession Elijah tells his servant to go and look toward the sea. His servant goes according to his master's command and reports back that there was nothing to see. Instead of giving up and walking away or assuming he had misheard the Lord, Elijah persists. Elijah continues before the Lord in prayer and intercession. Seven times we are told that this process was repeated of Elijah praying and sending his servant to report back to him what he saw.

> *And (Elijah) said to his servant, Go up now, look toward the sea. And he went up, and looked, and said, There is nothing. And he said, Go again seven times. And it came to pass at the seventh time, that he said, Behold, there ariseth a little cloud out of the sea, like a man's hand. And he said, Go up, say unto Ahab, Prepare thy chariot, and get thee down, that the rain stop thee not. (1Ki 18:43-44)*

Elijah would seek the Lord in prayer and intercession and then send his servant to check if the Lord had answered. For the first six times there was no answer. The Lord was silent and yet Elijah was not perturbed or dismayed. Elijah did not give up or get angry with the Lord. Elijah persisted understanding that the call to pray involved plurality of action. It was not a call to pray once, but a call to persist in pray.

The call to the people of God to pray is to press in, continually seeking the Lord to intervene and not giving up until we see Him move. God would have His people to

continue until they see the promised results coming on the horizon. His people are to pray with a faith that believes the Lord will hear them at the chosen place.
Elijah fervently prayed as one of, and also as a representative of, Gods people. The encouraging thing for believers is that James tells us in James 5:18 that:

> *Elijah was a man subject to like passions as we are, and he prayed earnestly that it might not rain: and it rained not on the earth by the space of three years and six months. And he prayed again, and the heaven gave rain, and the earth brought forth her fruit.(Jas 5:17-18)*

Elijah's prayer unto the Lord for the drought to end was not heard because he was the prophet of the Lord. Elijah was heard because he prayed in accordance with the word of God and continued praying until he saw that word realised. In every way Elijah was just like us, but he persisted in prayer even when he wasn't seeing results. Seven times Elijah turned to look for the cloud. Rather than give up, Elijah sets forth the example and the need for us to continue in prayer for those things that God has spoken to us about.

4. And seek My face

Elijah's life was dedicated to seeking the Lord. When everyone else had fallen away, the priority for Elijah was the Lord God. Throughout this chapter Elijah's priority is seeking the Lord.

> *Hear me, O LORD, hear me, that this people may know that thou art the LORD God, and that thou hast turned their heart back again.(1Ki 18:37)*

He seeks the Lord to answer his prayers and show Himself once more to the people. He then seeks the Lord in humility and persistent prayer for Him to end the drought, famine and pestilence in the land. Elijah's continual focus is on the Lord and seeking Him. Elijah's focus never strayed from looking upon the Lord. Everything he did was to not only draw himself closer to the Lord, but also draw the nation of Israel closer.

Elijah continually sought the face of the Lord and sought to ever go deeper in relationship with Him. For Israel they were about to start back on this path, having strayed from it and gone after Baal.

5. And turn from their wicked ways

The people of the Lord had long since turned their back on the Him. They had pursued after Baal and followed the lead of Ahab and Jezebel. When Elijah first addressed the people and prophets of Baal on Mount Carmel he posed two challenges to them. In the first one Elijah says:

Example

> *..... How long halt ye between two opinions? if the LORD be God, follow Him: but if Baal, then follow him. And the people answered him not a word. (1Ki 18:21)*

Notice here that the people were not willing to answer. They were not willing to turn from their wicked ways and leave Baal.

Elijah then outlines how they will determine who is actually God. He proposes essentially a challenge between the prophets of Baal and himself. The God who would answer by fire, He would be God. The people responded this time to Elijah, answering very simply, saying "It is well spoken". In other words, we are not going to make a choice and turn from anything until we see some evidence. There was no conviction in the people, no hint of turning from their wicked ways. The people of the Lord, bar Elijah, were well and truly compromised.

Once the test is carried out though and the Lord answers Elijah with fire, consuming the sacrifice, altar, water and dust we see the hearts of the people start to turn:
> *And when all the people saw it, they fell on their faces: and they said, The LORD, he is the God; the LORD, he is the God. (1Ki 18:39)*

The people were no longer double minded and turned from any belief in Baal to a solitary belief in the Lord as God. It is after this that the people continue the evidence of this and remove the wicked priests from the nation.

The hearts of the people turned back to the Lord. They turned from their wicked ways and once again set their faces to seek the Lord. All compromise was abolished and the people of the Lord turned from their wicked ways.

D. The Response

*And it came to pass at the seventh time, that he said, Behold, **there ariseth a little cloud** out of the sea, like a man's hand. And he said, Go up, say unto Ahab, Prepare thy chariot, and get thee down, that the rain stop thee not. And it came to pass **in the mean while, that the heaven was black with clouds and wind, and there was a great rain**. And Ahab rode, and went to Jezreel.(1Ki 18:44-45)*

After three and a half years of drought, which had led to famine and subsequent pestilence, the nation experienced relief from the judgement that had come upon it. The skies were black with clouds and great rain was poured out across the land. This was no ordinary outpouring, this was a supernatural outpouring of rain by the Lord.

It is to be noted that this response of the Lord came after:

1. His people called by His name
2. Had humbled themselves

3. Elijah had prayed
4. Elijah sought the face of the Lord
5. The people of the Lord had turned from their Wicked Ways

The "If" conditions had been met and it was "Then" that the Lord heard from heaven, forgave their sin and healed their land. The Lord responded because the people returned.

> He **Turns** in response to the **Turn** of His people
> He **Hears** in response to the **Words** of His people
> He **Forgives** in response to the **Repentance** of His people
> He **Heals** in response to the **Plea** of His people
> He fulfils the **Then** when His people fulfil the **If**

God is ever faithful to His Word, but once again we see that the onus lays with His people. The Lord is ever faithful with His response, the determining factor lies with the people called by His name.

E. The Promise

When the Lord chooses a place through the provision of His Holy sanctifying fire His promise is that His attention will be on that place. We see in this example that the Lord had chosen Mount Carmel when His fire fell from heaven, consuming the sacrifice of Elijah. We go on to see the promise of the Lord in relation to the chosen place fulfilled as He responds to the actions and prayers of His people, sending rain upon the Land. The Lord's eyes were open to see the actions of His people and His ears were open to hear their prayer.

The focus of the Lord was upon His chosen place. That which He promised in 2 Chronicles 7 is evidenced here. His promise is confirmed and proven in this example. That which He spoke forth in Chronicles is witnessed and attested to in 1 Kings. The eyes and ears of the Lord are ever attuned to His chosen place and His people who seek him in prayer and with sacrifice there.

If My People

EXAMPLE SUMMARY

In the example we have just looked at from 1 Kings 18 we saw the scriptural account of Elijah's encounter with the prophets of Baal and the events that surrounded this. As we studied this example, we have seen the truths that we discovered in 2 Chronicles 7 demonstrated.

A. <u>The Chosen Place</u>
The chosen place of the Lord in this case was Mount Carmel. In response to the prayer and cry of Elijah the Lord poured out His divine fire upon Mount Carmel, consuming the altar, sacrifice, water and dust. We see here the Lord's choice and acceptance of His chosen place through the provision of Holy fire. It was because of this choice and acceptance by the Lord that Elijah returned here to pray for the cessation of the judgements of God on the nation of Israel.

We further saw the confirmation of the linkage between the chosen place, prayer and sacrifice. The three are interconnected.

B. <u>The Judgements</u>
Elijah had initially declared that the heavens would be shut upon Israel in judgement for the nations backsliding. This drought continued for three and a half years and during this time its effects grew as seen in the further judgements from the Lord. We see here the three judgements of the Lord:
1. No rain – Heavens were shut for three and a half years causing drought and the waterways to dry up. 1 Kings 17:1, 1 Kings 18:1
2. Locusts – Famine, oppression, lack of provision. Ahab and his servant searched out the land in the hope of finding some feed for the cattle. There was not enough – 1 Kings 18:2
3. Pestilence – Death. Some of the livestock had already passed away and the King was desperate to try and save what remained – 1 Kings 18:5

These three judgements were progressive. What started as drought lead to famine which lead to death. Nothing though was able to capture the attention of the people and bring them back to the Lord.

C. <u>The People</u>
In 1 Kings 18 The Lord was calling to the nation of Israel. It is Elijah and the people of Israel who are His chosen people in this example. At this point in time Judah was under a Godly King, but Israel had turned from the Lord under the rule and example of Ahab and Jezebel. It is upon Mount Carmel we learn:
1. His people called by His name
2. Humbled themselves – 1 Kings 18:39, 42

Example Summary

3. Elijah Prayed – 1 Kings 18:42
4. Elijah sought His face – 1 Kings 18:43
5. They turned from their wicked ways – 1 Kings 18:39

There is no mistaking the return to the Lord that occurred here. The people of Israel, the people of God, repented of their pride and humbled themselves before the living God. They fulfilled the "If" conditions.

D. <u>The Response</u>

The Lord shows that He hears the intercessory prayers of Elijah and witnessed the repentance of the people by responding with a supernatural outpouring of rain upon the nation.

1. He shows that He hears.
2. He shows that He forgives.
3. He shows that He heals.

The rain from heaven ended the drought and brought healing to the land, bringing an end to the famine and pestilence. The Lord heard the prayer of Elijah, He forgave the sins of the people and He sent rain to heal the land.

E. <u>The Promise</u>

The Lord's eyes were upon and His ears were attentive to His chosen place. He saw and heard what occurred at His chosen place. He fulfilled His promise from 2 Chronicles 7.

SUMMARY OF EXPOSITION AND EXAMPLE

In 2 Chronicles 7 we started with our exposition and then moved on to consider the example of Elijah in 1 Kings 18. In order to try and re-enforce the truths that we have discovered in both of these accounts we will quickly recap what we have learned so far.

A. The Chosen Place

We see between these two scriptural accounts that the chosen place was not a constant. What started off as the Temple of Solomon in Chronicles became Mount Carmel for Elijah in 1 Kings. What unites both however is the divine fire of the Lord. God is not bound by material buildings or monuments, God is far bigger than that. God shows us through these accounts that His choice is shown by the provision of Holy fire. This fire declares His choice and acceptance and points to where His people are to pray.

We also see through these two accounts the interconnectedness of the chosen place, prayer and sacrifice. These three things are interwoven and bound together.

2 Chronicles 7	1 Kings 18
Temple of Solomon	Mount Carmel
Fire of the Lord fell	Fire of the Lord fell
Consumed the sacrifice	Consumed the sacrifice, altar, water and dust
Showed the Lord's acceptance and choice	Showed the Lords acceptance and Choice
After this the Lord declared this was where His people where to pray when His judgements were in the Land	After this Elijah prayed for the Lord to relent from His judgements on the Land
Place of heard prayer	The prayers of Elijah were heard here
Place of sacrifice	Sacrifice was made upon the altar Elijah rebuilt
Chosen Place, Prayer and Sacrifice connected - vs 12	Chosen Place, Prayer and Sacrifice connected - vs 36-38

B. The Judgements

In 2 Chronicles 7 we read that the Lord outlines three judgements that would fall on His people. In 1 Kings 18 we see these three judgements in action

2 Chronicles 7	1 Kings 18
Shut up heaven that there be no rain – drought	The rains were shut up for three and a half years – Israel was in drought
If I command locusts to devour the land – lack of provision, oppression, famine	The land was in famine – lack of provision, oppression, famine
Or if I send pestilence, death	Loss of livestock, death

Summary of Exposition and Example

In the time of Elijah, Israel was experiencing the judgements the Lord had forewarned of in 2 Chronicles 7. They were experiencing the progressive nature of the judgements of the Lord and feeling the effects of this as they kept on their path away from the Lord. What started as a shut heaven had lead to locusts and was now at a state of pestilence within the land.

C. The People

The people the Lord refers to in both accounts are those that are called by His name. It is to the children of God that He refers and it is upon them that the onus is placed to return unto Him. It is not to heathen nations or unbelievers, but unto His children that the call goes out to. In both accounts God is calling to the children of Israel. As He calls, we see that the Lord lays out conditions for His people to meet. These formed the 'If' conditions.

2 Chronicles 7	1 Kings 18
My people – the children of God, the united houses of Israel and Judah	My People – Elijah and the nation of Israel
Will Humble themselves	Elijah falls before the Lord The people fall on their faces
Pray	Elijah prayed repeatedly for the Lord to intercede
Seek my face	Elijah sought the face of the Lord
Turn from their wicked ways	The people turned from their Idol worship and divided hearts

These "If" conditions are the responsibility of His children to fulfil. It is their responsibility and theirs alone. The onus lies with the people of God.

D. The Response

If the people of the Lord would fulfil their "If" conditions "Then" He would respond. We see this truth confirmed in these two passages. We see the response that the Lord promises in 2 Chronicles come to pass in 1 Kings after the people returned unto Him.

2 Chronicles 7	1 Kings 18
I will hear from heaven	The Lord heard the prayer of Elijah
I will forgive their sin	He forgave the sins of the people when they humbled themselves before Him
I will heal their land	He sent rain to heal the land
Judgement to Blessing	Judgement to Blessing
Promise of the Lord	Promise fulfilled

When His people fulfil their part the Lord fulfils His and hears, forgives and heals.

E. The Promise

The promise of the Lord is that His eyes will ever be upon and His ears ever attentive to His chosen place. He promised this to Solomon and we see this promise fulfilled in the example of Elijah. Whilst the sites varied, the promise of the Lord was shown to be fulfilled at His chosen place. The chosen place is a place that the Lord focuses on and looks for a response from His people at.

Final Thoughts

In 2 Chronicles 7 we see a declaration from the Lord in response to the prayer of Solomon. The Lord here declares that when His judgements are in the earth His people are to seek Him at His chosen place and if they will do that then He will respond. In 1 Kings 18 we see the effects of these judgements in action and we see that the Lord responds to these when His people truly seek Him at the chosen place, according to the ways He has outlined, and brings healing to the land.

What we further discovered was the importance of the chosen place in this and whilst this had changed between 2 Chronicles 7 and 1 Kings 18, the Lord always demonstrated His chosen place in the same way. The Lord shows His divine choice through the provision of Holy fire from heaven. Whilst the Lord may change the place, it is up to the people of the Lord to understand how the Lord displays His choice and acceptance. Elijah understood this and that is why he didn't return to the temple of Solomon to pray as 1 Kings 18 highlights. He understood what the fire of the Lord meant and that is why he ascended Mount Carmel to seek the Lord for the cessation of His judgements.

We have also seen how the chosen place, prayer and sacrifice are interwoven and linked in both scriptural accounts. The place that the Lord chooses through the provision of His holy fire is to be a place of prayer and sacrifice. The connection of these three is of vital importance.

It is this same understanding that we need to keep at the forefront of our minds as we move into our next section and look at the application of all this to us as believers and corporately as the Church. We have seen the truths revealed in 2 Chronicles 7. We have seen the truth exemplified in 1 Kings 18. As we move forward, we will see these truths in application.

APPLICATION

How does all this apply to the Church and the modern day believer?

Having looked at our sections on Exposition and Example we now turn our attention to the application of truths from 2 Chronicles 7. We have seen how the truths revealed in 2 Chronicles were confirmed by the events in 1 Kings 18. We now look at how these truths apply to the Church and the believers who form it. It is the writer's firm belief that this is a message that the Lord would have us grab hold of.

Our focus here is the Church, particularly those events surrounding it's birth. As we focus in on the Church we will hopefully see how these truths apply to New Testament believers. Before we continue though we must first consider two points that will aid us in seeing how the truths will apply to the Church and the believer.

BACKGROUND

In Acts Chapter 2 we read of what has been deemed the birth of the Church in the New Testament. Here as the disciples were gathered together in an upper room on the day of Pentecost in unity and of one accord, the Lord poured out his Holy Spirit upon them, according to the words of Jesus. Tongues of fire fell and His Spirit filled the room that they were gathered in. The disciples started speaking in other tongues as the Spirit gave them utterance. This caused no small stir amongst all of the Israelites that had gathered in Jerusalem for the feast of Pentecost at that time. Some of the people presumed them to be drunk. Peter in response to this, and under inspiration of the Holy Spirit, launched into his famous sermon. He exhorted the people on what was happening and preached to them the message of Jesus. Three thousand people received the words of Peter and were baptised that day. These individuals were added to the Church and continued steadfastly in the apostle's doctrine, as well as fellowship and the breaking of bread. The New Testament Church was born. From this chapter of Acts it is evidenced:

A. The people repented
B. They were baptised
C. They received the Holy Spirit
D. They continued steadfastly in the apostle's doctrine
E. They continued in fellowship
F. They continued in prayer
G. They broke bread together

Application

This was truly the birth and foundation of the New Testament Church and as the days progressed Acts 2:47 tells us that:

> *Praising God, and having favour with all the people. And the Lord added to the Church daily such as should be saved. (Act 2:47)*

This was indeed a new thing in the nation of Israel, and the world, but it is something that had long been foretold. The Church was born on the great day of Pentecost and the Lord continued to grow it in the days that followed. The reader is encouraged to read Acts 2 before moving forward in this section.

NATURAL AND SPIRITUAL APPLICATION

As we move into this section we will see the truths of a biblical principle that can be found in 1 Corinthians 15:46.

> *Howbeit that was not first which is spiritual, but that which is natural; and afterward that which is spiritual. (1Co 15:46)*

This principle states that God often demonstrate truths in the Old Testament in the natural before revealing the spiritual application of these truths in the New Testament. In simple summary it is, first the natural and then the spiritual. The Old Testament gives us the natural example and truths and the New Testament gives us the spiritual reality and application of these truths.

An example of this can be found with the act of circumcision. God introduced the natural act of circumcision unto the nation of Israel which set them apart from the other nations of the world. It was a physical act performed in the natural upon all the men of Israel.

In the New Testament though, it is not the natural act of circumcision but the spiritual application that is emphasised.

> *For he is not a Jew, which is one outwardly; neither is that circumcision, which is outward in the flesh: But he is a Jew, which is one inwardly; and circumcision is that of the heart, in the spirit, and not in the letter; whose praise is not of men, but of God. (Rom 2:28-29)*

In the Old Testament it was the natural act that God laid down with its truths. But in the New Testament we see the spiritual realities of these applied. Circumcision was once an act in the natural, but God takes the truths that the natural revealed and applies them to the spiritual reality. God takes the natural example from the Old Testament and applies those truths to the spiritual reality in the New Testament. God no longer looks on the natural state of man, but on his spiritual state revealed by the condition of his heart. It is the circumcised heart of man that sets him apart as one of the people of God.

The natural points to the spiritual. It is first the natural and then the spiritual. God does this because by nature man is able to comprehend natural things. He uses these natural things to explain truths that He then applies to the spiritual. One only has to read the parables of Jesus to see countless examples of this. God bridges the gap of man's understanding by communicating to him in a way that he can understand. He introduces the natural to lay the foundation for the spiritual.

It is with this thought that we move into this section. As we progress through this Application section we will see both the natural and spiritual application of the truths of the Lord from 2 Chronicles. Here we will see the same format as our previous sections in order to best communicate the truths that God is speaking forth through His Word.

A. The Chosen Place
Our focus for this point is Acts 2:1-4. In order to understand this fully we will spend a little time exploring the specifics of this passage, before looking at our points associated with the chosen place

And when the day of Pentecost was fully come, (Act 2:1)

Pentecost was the second of the three great feasts of Israel. There was the feast of Passover, the feast of Pentecost and the feast of Tabernacles. The Lord Jesus gave himself on the cross of Calvary during the feast of Passover and now some two months later the disciples would experience the outpouring of the Holy Spirit during the feast of Pentecost and the Church would be born.

They were all with one accord in one place. (Act 2:1)

Expositors take these to be more than just the apostles of the Lord. Most take this to be the one hundred and twenty disciples mentioned in Acts 1:15. These one hundred and twenty were gathered together. They were not just in one place, but they were also of one accord. This was a unified gathering.

And suddenly there came a sound from heaven as of a rushing mighty wind, and it filled all the house where they were sitting. (Act 2:2)

The wind is a symbol of the Holy Spirit. Here the sound was heard coming from heaven and filled the house where the one hundred and twenty were gathered. The wind of the Lord filled the house. It blew over all who were in the house gathered in unity.

And there appeared unto them cloven tongues like as of fire, and it sat upon each of them (Act 2:3)

Application

There appeared cloven tongues like of fire. They heard the wind, but they saw the fire. These tongues of fire appeared in the room and then descended upon each of the one hundred and twenty disciples.

And they were all filled with the Holy Ghost, (Act 2:4)

When the tongues sat upon each disciple they were immediately filled with the Holy Ghost. The presence of the Lord had filled the house with the wind and now the presence of the Lord filled the disciples as the tongues of fire descended upon them.

To be filled with the Holy Spirit is to be consumed by Him. Everything else falls away as the Spirit fills our mortal bodies. The disciples here were consumed by the Holy Spirit. They had given themselves to seeking the Lord, according to the words of Jesus. They were literally living sacrifices and here the Lord comes down with His fire from heaven and consumes them. This was no partial distribution, each of the disciples was filled with the Spirit.

and began to speak with other tongues, as the Spirit gave them utterance. (Act 2:4)

The spiritual tongues of fire that landed effected their native tongues. This was a spiritual encounter that had natural effects. The anointing of the Lord overrode any natural abilities and allowed the tongues of the disciples to speak in languages that they weren't fluent in. As they spoke under the anointing of the Spirit, those from other countries that could hear them understood the message that was being spoken in their native tongue.

1. The Place

We have seen through our Exposition and Example that the Lord demonstrates His choice and acceptance through the provision of the His Holy fire. We see that same truth evidenced here. The Lord here pours out His Holy fire on His chosen place. This chosen place was not the one hundred and twenty disciples. It was not where they were gathered. Rather it is what they represented. The one hundred and twenty disciples were the Church at that time. They were the disciples of the Lord who had repented of their sins, accepted Jesus as their saviour and had been baptised in water. This was the New Testament Church and here the Lord pours out His Holy Spirit in the form of tongues of fire to not only anoint the one hundred and twenty disciples with the promised Holy Spirit but to also highlight to us that the Church is now His chosen place. The chosen place is no longer a building or a mountain but it is a spiritual gathering. The Lord used the natural in the Old Testament to point towards what He would do in the spiritual in the New Testament. The Church is believers gathered together in unity and it is this that is the chosen place of the Lord. The Church is a spiritual house formed when believers gather together in unity. Whilst we may meet in buildings, houses, stadiums etc, it is never the place that makes a Church. It is the Lords people together gathered together in unity that is the chosen place. Scripture tells us that:

For where two or three are gathered together in my name, there am I in the midst of them. (Mat 18:20)

It is the coming together in unity of His people that forms the Church and it is this gathering that the Lord shows forth on the day of Pentecost in Acts Chapter 2 to be His chosen place. The Lord shows us this through the provision of His Holy fire upon the one hundred and twenty disciples.

2. The Place of Prayer

The Church is the New Testament House of God and the cry of Jesus was that His house was to be a House of prayer.

And said unto them, It is written, My house shall be called the house of prayer; but ye have made it a den of thieves. (Mat 21:13)

The call is for the Church to be a people of prayer and to be serious about it. The Church is to be as Elijah and stand in the gap for the nations, seeking the Lord for His mercy on the judgements in our nations, natural and spiritual. Elijah interceded for his nation and this is the call to the Church of today. The Church is to be a house of fervent prayer. A place where the people of the Lord truly press into the Lord for His intervention into the state of the world around us. It requires His people to be passionate and dedicated. It requires us to have the heart of Elijah (1 Ki 18:43) and the persistent widow (Luk 18:1-8) and keep coming before the Lord until we see His intervention. It is to break all forms of apathy and chase the Father with fervent intention to see His blessings flow forth.

Prayer should not just be something that bookends our meetings and services. The Church is to be saturated with the fragrant smell of the prayers of the saints that rise as incense to the Father (Rev 8:4). Our gatherings need the power of prayer. As the Church steps up and becomes the House of prayer that Jesus spoke of, we will see the power of God unleashed on earth.

3. The Place of Sacrifice

As we noted above, on the day of Pentecost when the tongues of fire fell upon the one hundred and twenty disciples they were filled with the Holy Spirit. The fire of the Lord descends and consumes (fills) the one hundred and twenty disciples as living sacrifices. The Old Testament truths point to the New Testament reality. What was once a natural act where the people of Israel would present an offering to the Lord is now fulfilled by His people presenting themselves as living sacrifices unto Him. Pauls call in Romans is:

I beseech you therefore, brethren, by the mercies of God, that ye present your bodies a living sacrifice, holy, acceptable unto God, which is your reasonable service. (Rom 12:1)

Application

As the one hundred and twenty presented themselves, the fire of the Lord fell and consumed these living sacrifices. As believers we are called to take up our cross and follow Jesus (Matt 16:24). We are called to live a life of sacrifice unto Him who was our sacrifice.

This truth has particular application as we come together at the chosen place. Whenever we come together, forming the Church, we are to come as sacrifices unto Him. Everything is to be about Him. Our focus, our priority, our wants and desires should all be focused on Him and completely off ourselves. We come as a sacrifice unto Him at the place He has chosen. We bring ourselves unto Him, presenting ourselves upon the spiritual altar. The focus is on giving, giving ourselves unto Him according to His Word.

The truths that we discovered from our Exposition and Example now apply to the Church. We see the exact same truths, but with a spiritual application.

2 Chronicles 7	1 Kings 18	Acts 2
Temple of Solomon	Mount Carmel	The Upper Room
Great Gathering – dedication of the temple	Great Gathering – All Israel assembled	Great gathering – Feast of Pentecost
Solomon	Elijah	The one hundred and twenty disciples
Offering and Sacrifice	Offering and Sacrifice	Living sacrifices
Glory filled the House		Upper room filled with the wind of the Spirit
Fire of the Lord	Fire of the Lord	Fire of the Lord
Fire descended	Fire descended	Fire descended
Consumed the offerings and sacrifices	Consumed the offerings and sacrifice	Consumed the living sacrifices – the disciples filled
Natural House	Natural Mountain	Spiritual House
The Temple of Solomon – The House of God		The Church – The House of God
The Chosen Place	The Chosen Place	The Chosen Place
The Place of Heard Prayer	The Place of Heard Prayer	The Place of Heard Prayer
The Place of Sacrifice	The Place of Sacrifice	The Place of Sacrifice

The Church is the spiritual fulfilment of the truths that the Lord revealed in 2 Chronicles 7 and 1 Kings 18. We see in Acts Chapter 2 that the fire of the Lord falls upon the one hundred and twenty disciples, filling them with the Holy Spirit and showing to us that the Lords chosen place in the New Testament is His spiritual house, the Church. Acts 2 reveals to us that the Church is the chosen place of the Lord. The Church is the place that the Lord has chosen and it is the Church that is to be the place of prayer and the place of sacrifice. The three are interconnected and are to be evident in the Church today. The truths that the Temple of Solomon and Mt Carmel spoke of are to be fulfilled in the Church.

B. The Judgements

Throughout our Exposition and Example we looked at the natural judgements that are detailed in 2 Chronicles 7 and 1 Kings 18. There we discovered that there were three progressive judgements of the Lord listed in Chronicles and confirmed in Kings. As a refresher these were:

2 Chronicles 7	1 Kings 18
Shut up heaven that there be no rain – drought	The rains were shut up for three and a half years – Israel was in drought
If I command locusts to devour the land – lack of provision	The land was in famine – lack of provision, oppression, people impoverished
Or if I send pestilence	Loss of livestock

There is absolutely no doubt that we still see the evidence of these judgements in effect in our days, but as we have already discussed the natural truths of these examples also point to spiritual realities. Whilst we still experience these natural judgements of drought, famine and pestilence we also experience their spiritual counterparts. Throughout our sections on Exposition and Example we have already discussed the natural judgements in great detail so here we will solely focus on the spiritual application of these.

1. No Rain – Shut Heaven

Rain points to the blessing of God poured out from heaven. It is symbolic of His Holy Spirit and His Word. The provision of rain speaks of revival, refreshing and an outpouring of the Word and the Spirit. Consider the following verses:

> *Give ear, O ye heavens, and I will speak; and hear, O earth, the words of my mouth.* ***My doctrine shall drop as the rain, my speech shall distil as the dew,*** *as the small rain upon the tender herb, and as the showers upon the grass:(Deu 32:1-2)*

> ***For as the rain cometh down****, and the snow from heaven, and returneth not thither, but watereth the earth, and maketh it bring forth and bud, that it may give seed to the sower, and bread to the eater:* **So shall my word be that goeth forth out of my mouth***: it shall not return unto me void, but it shall accomplish that which I please, and it shall prosper in the thing whereto I sent it.(Isa 55:10-11)*

> *And it shall come to pass afterward, that* ***I will pour out my spirit*** *upon all flesh; and your sons and your daughters shall prophesy, your old men shall dream dreams, your young men shall see visions: (Joe 2:28)*

Application

Come, and let us return unto the LORD: for he hath torn, and he will heal us; he hath smitten, and he will bind us up. After two days will he revive us: in the third day he will raise us up, and we shall live in his sight. Then shall we know, if we follow on to know the LORD: his going forth is prepared as the morning; and **he shall come unto us as the rain**, *as the latter and former rain unto the earth. (Hos 6:1-3)*

Just as natural rain provides refreshment and nourishment to the natural world, so to do the spiritual rains of the Lord have similar effects. The spiritual rains speak of the Lord pouring out of His Word and His Spirit upon His people. These rains are for the refreshment, nourishment and to aid the growth of the people of the Lord. To have no rain would speak of a lack of His Word and His Spirit. It refers to the outpouring of His Word and His Spirit being withheld from the people of God, causing dryness and a thirst that cannot be quenched through natural means. When the heavens are shut in the spiritual the people of the Lord miss the blessing of His Spirit and Word being poured out.

Just as with a shut heaven in the natural though, the effects do not stop here. The same truth applies with the spiritual, a lack of rain will lead to a drought. Shut heavens eventually lead to a spiritual drought and spiritual drought leads to the decline of spiritual life. All life needs water in order to be sustained. The spiritual rains of the Lord through the outpouring of His Word and Spirit bring revelation and nourishment to the people of God. It is these outpourings that allow His people to dissect and understand the meat of the Word and to press deeper in the Spirit through an increased understanding. As He pours out His Church receives revelation and truth which causes the people of the Lord to grow in spiritual life. The rain waters the seed and causes it to grow to maturity. As the Lord pours out His Word and His Spirit upon His people, His people grow in understanding and revelation of Him, His Spirit and His Word. We grow up, we go deeper and we mature as believers collectively. The spiritual rains cause the spiritual crops to grow which provide for His people. Open heavens are not only a blessing for the people of God to bask in, they cause the spiritual growth of the people of the Lord. The spiritual rains cause spiritual life to flourish. His people need the rains of the Lord for their spiritual lives to thrive.

When the Heavens are shut, drought comes onto the scene and life is affected. Spiritual rain causes the spiritual man to flourish, but spiritual drought causes the spiritual life of the body of Christ to decline. Spiritual drought effects man and his spiritual growth, it effects the spiritual life of the people of God. A shut heaven leads to spiritual decline for the people of the Lord through a lack of provision of spiritual nourishment. We need the water of His Word and Spirit to sustain our spiritual life. It is the outpouring of His rains that causes spiritual growth within His people. The spiritual life of the Church is effected when there are no rains of the Lord. When His Word and His Spirit dry up, His people cannot grow up and they begin to decline due to a lack of spiritual rain.

If My People

Shut heavens effect the spiritual life of the people of God.

2.   Locusts – Famine, Oppression, Impoverishment
The locust comes after the drought and consumes the little that is left. In a spiritual sense it speaks of the people of God being overrun, oppressed and impoverished through the enemy seeking to take the little provision that they have left after the spiritual drought.

Just as the natural body requires provision to live and grow so too does the spiritual body. Spiritual locusts speak of the Church being oppressed and impoverished in order to take the last remnants of spiritual life that have survived the drought. It points to the people of God being in a state of famine.

In the writer's mind this would point to a lack of the Word of God. The Word of God is compared to bread and manna. The manna which fed the nation of Israel during their wilderness wonderings points to the spiritual provision of the Lord to His people of His Word. A spiritual famine points to a lack of provision of spiritual bread. Famine doesn't necessarily mean a complete lack of provision, but it does mean having a very limited amount of provision. It can be enough to survive but certainly not enough to thrive. Crumbs can help an appetite but they are not the same as the nourishment a loaf of bread provides. (Mat 15:27, Luk 16:21)

The judgement of locusts points to the people of the Lord starving from a lack of the Word of God. Spiritual locusts devour the little that is left from the spiritual drought. The spiritual locusts seek to attack the remaining spiritual sustenance of the people of God. This judgement continues the downward spiral of the spiritual life of His people. The spiritual locusts seek to take hope from the Church and cause a state of starvation amongst His people. It is something that further weakens the spiritual state of the people of the Lord.

We need to keep in mind though, that the judgements of the Lord we are considering come with the purpose of drawing His people back to Him. The spiritual hunger felt by the people of God caused by the plague of spiritual locusts should point them back to the Lord. It should highlight to them the need they have of the true manna from heaven.

3.   Pestilence
My people are destroyed for lack of knowledge: because thou hast rejected knowledge, I will also reject thee, that thou shalt be no priest to me: seeing thou hast forgotten the law of thy God, I will also forget thy children. (Hos 4:6)

Pestilence in the natural speaks of death. Spiritual pestilence speaks of spiritual death. Where there is no rain and no provision the spiritual state of the people of the Lord starts to decline. It is the natural progression of the first two judgements. Where spiritual life

Application

is not nourished it diminishes. Just as natural man needs food and water so too does spiritual man need spiritual food and spiritual water. When spiritual man is not nourished he begins to head down the path to pestilence.

If the people of the Lord do not respond to the hunger and thirst caused by the first two judgments of the Lord then they will find themselves in a state of spiritual pestilence. If the cries of spiritual man for nourishment are continually supressed, dismissed and ignored then the natural progression is spiritual death.

The natural judgements of God in the earth experienced by His people where always a result of His people turning away from Him. So it is with the spiritual. The spiritual judgements of God are seen when His people turn from Him. Again it should be noted here the progressive nature of these judgements. First comes a drought in the rains of God. Next comes a lack in spiritual food. And finally spiritual death comes upon His people. What starts as spiritual drought will lead to spiritual famine and end in spiritual death if we do not turn back. Just as the natural body needs food and water to survive so does the spiritual body need spiritual water and spiritual food to survive.

So whilst the natural judgements of the Lord are still seen in the earth today it is vital that the Church also be aware of the spiritual judgements of the Lord as well.

Natural	Spiritual
Drought – No Rain	Lack of the outpouring of the Holy spirit and Word
Locusts - Famine	Lack in the Word (bread) of God
Pestilence	Spiritual Death

C. The People

In our previous sections we have seen how this call and the responsibilities that go with it have rested upon natural Israel. Having discovered the chosen place is now the Church we now look at to who this call and the "If" responsibilities that go with it apply to.

1. If My people who are called by My name
*And when he had found him, he brought him unto Antioch. And it came to pass, that a whole year they assembled themselves with the Church, and taught much people. And the disciples were called **Christians** first in Antioch. (Act 11:26)*
The call remains the same, it is to the people of God. It is not to natural Israel though, but to spiritual Israel. We are His people through belief and acceptance of Jesus as our Lord and Saviour. It is through this that we bear the name Christians. As Christians we are His people called by His name, Christ. We bear the name of Christ and are called by it. The Church consists of His people called by His name.

The Lord does not look on our natural heritage, but on our spiritual heritage. It is through Christ that we are accounted as His children and His people.

> *There is neither Jew nor Greek, there is neither bond nor free, there is neither male nor female: for ye are all one in Christ Jesus. (Gal 3:28)*

To be called a Christian is to be called by His name. It is through Christ that we are made members of the family of God and having done this we take upon ourselves the responsibility of this call. The call that once rested upon natural Israel now applies to spiritual Israel. Paul in Romans when explaining how God has opened up His call to the gentiles quotes an incredible verse from Hosea:

> *As he saith also in Osee (Hosea), I will call them **my people**, which were not **my people**; and her beloved, which was not beloved. And it shall come to pass, that in the place where it was said unto them, Ye are not my people; there shall they be called the children of the living God. (Rom 9:25-26)*

The call that was once restricted to Natural Israel is now open to any who accept the Lord Jesus Christ as the saviour It is through Him that we become part of His people called by His name.

The call of My people belongs to the Church and the believers who form it. The responsibility of the "If" belongs to us. We are now the people.

2. Shall Humble themselves

In our Exposition we noted that humility is not only the recognition of a greater power, but coming under His authority and acknowledging our need of and seeking His help and intervention.

One of the problems for the people of God, particularly in the western world, is that we have so many ways of meeting our own needs. This ability to meet our own needs can leave us apathetic to our need of God. We readily have hospitals and doctors available to meet any of the health concerns we have. Food is available from any number of local stores and never in short supply Drinking water flows freely from our taps. We have credit cards and other means to cover any cash shortfalls we may have. Our desperation levels are relatively low and with this a sense of apathy can arise where we don't really see the need for the Lord's help in given situations. It is not necessarily that we are proud it is just that our level of need can be low. The only way to change this to have a change in mindset.

The Lord would have us come to Him as He outlines in Mathew 18:4:

> *Whosoever therefore shall humble himself as this little child, the same is greatest in the kingdom of heaven. (Mat 18:4)*

Application

A child looks to their parent as their unequivocal source of provision because they totally are dependent upon them. The Lord would have His people look upon Him in the same way. He would have us look beyond ourselves and how we can meet our own needs and look to Him and see how abundantly more He can meet them. The problem with apathy is that it can actually cause us to be content with situations that are less than what the Father would have for us. Paul learned to be content in any situation because he understood the state he was in was from the Lord. But many of us have learned to be content in any state, even if it is not the fulness of what the Lord would have for us.

For the Church to humble itself it must by necessity understand the fulness of what the Lord has for it and then in childlike faith humbly seek Him for the fulfillment of that. Humility flows out from of an understanding that the Lord has more for His Church and that He is the only one who can provide what is lacking. When we have that understanding and attitude in our heart we readily fall before the Lord in desperation. We fall in humility for our reliance is completely on Him and we understand that it is solely by His grace that we may receive what we need.

For the Church and the people of God to humble themselves they:

- a) Must break the attitude of apathy
- b) Understand the fulness of what the Lord has for His Church and His people
- c) Understand that His fulness for us is undeserved and unearned
- d) Understand that He alone can provide for our needs.

We are to come to the Father with the wide-eyed humility of a child looking to Him as the sole source of our provision.

3. And Pray

The call for the Church and for His people is to be a house/people of prayer. The Church, as the chosen place of God, is where prayer is to be made by His people. Upon humbling ourselves and recognising our need of Gods help, we then turn to Him in prayer and fervently seek the Lord for His answers, standing in the gap and interceding for those around us. Like we saw in our Exposition and Example, when we seek the Lord in prayer we are to do it at the chosen place, which as we discovered in Acts 2 is the Church.

We must remember here that the Church is a spiritual building, the Church is formed when two or three gather together in His name. The call is for His people to gather as the Church and pray. The gathering of His people is the chosen place and it is when this occurs that we are to pray to the Father as a collective. Whenever we come together in His name, prayer is to be at the forefront of what we do.

When the judgements of the Lord are evident in the world, whether they be natural or spiritual, the Church is to pray. The Church is too:

If My People

a) Pray for Rain
   1) Natural
   The Church is called to respond to issues such as natural drought. Rain in the natural and the spiritual is a blessing from God. If these aren't being experienced, then the people of the Lord need to seek the Father for these. Drought in instances may well be a judgement from the Lord, but the responsibility to seek the Lord for rain to end the drought lies with the Church.

   1) Spiritual
   It is not the writer's view that His people are in a spiritual drought, but nor is it the writer's belief that we are living in the fulness of God's blessing. The writer would put forward the following for the readers consideration. In Joel 2 we read of the rains of the Lord:

   > *Be glad then, ye children of Zion, and rejoice in the LORD your God: for he hath given you the former rain moderately, and he will cause to come down for you the rain, the former rain, and the latter rain in the first month. (Joe 2:23)*

   Here the Lord says that He has given the former rain moderately BUT He will cause the rain to come down, the former rain and the latter rain together. For the nation of Israel they would have the early rains and then there would be a dry period until the latter rains came. There were two distinct and separate periods of rain. The Church has experienced the early or former rains. These occurred in the early Church as the Spirit was poured out and great revelation of the Word came to His people. There remains however a promise to the Church, a great out pouring of rain. The Church has experienced some showers, but it is the writer's belief that we have not yet experienced the fulness of this. So whilst there may not be drought neither is there the fulness of rain that the Lord has promised. The call for the Church is that of Zechariah:

   > *Ask ye of the LORD rain in the time of the latter rain; so the LORD shall make bright clouds, and give them showers of rain, to every one grass in the field. (Zec 10:1)*

   The Church is to press into the Lord in prayer for the fulness of what He has for us. We are to pray for spiritual rain. The Church needs to see His Spirit and His Word rain down upon our nations. We need that blessing. We have had a taste and some pre-showers, but there remains yet an outpouring for the Church "If" we will seek the Father for it.

   The rains not only provide refreshment, they also allow the spiritual state of man to flourish with life. As the Lord pours out His Word and Spirit upon Man with

Application

His spiritual rains, man receives revelation and insight in the Word and in the Spirit. The rains provide a harvest for spiritual man to feed off allowing him to grow and mature in the fulness of what the Lord has for him. We need to pray for the rains not only for the blessing of refreshing but for the harvest of spiritual life they produce.

The Kingdom of Heaven is likened to seed by Jesus which is planted in the hearts of men. In order for this seed to grow it needs not only the right soil, it needs the blessing of rain. As the rain pours out, the plants grow and mature to the point where they bring forth fruit. This is what the Church needs. It needs not only the rain but also the growth that the rains bring, causing growth to occur and fruit to populate.
The spiritual life of the Church and His people is fuelled by the rains that He blesses us with.

b)   Pray against locusts
　　1)   Natural

We are to pray against famine. We are to pray for the land to produce. We are to pray for God's blessing upon the nations in which we live. Since the fall of man the ground has been cursed and it is by the sweat of man's brow it brings forth produce. The Church is to pray for its regions for the blessing and provision of God. We are to bind those things which would affect the ability of the land to produce and pray for God's blessing upon it.

　　1)   Spiritual

We have already discussed that in the natural and spiritual locusts come to take the little that remains after a drought and impoverish and oppress a nation, removing hope. Spiritually it speaks of the Church being starved of the Word.

As the people of the Lord we need to remember that when Jesus teaches his disciples to pray, part of the prayer reads:

Give us this day our daily bread. (Mat 6:11)

This no doubt has natural implications, but it also most definitely has spiritual application as well. From this we can discern that that there exists a daily provision of spiritual bread for every believer. Give us this day our daily bread. Not each week or fortnight, but each day there is daily bread.

We see the truth of this with the children of Israel and the manna in the wilderness. Whilst Israel wandered in the wilderness for forty years the Lord daily provided manna every morning for the people. Each morning the people would go out and collect an omer of manna for every person in their house. This manna was provided daily, but it was the responsibility of the people to get up and collect it. For the people of the Lord this involved a number of things:

i) They had to believe the Lord had daily provision for them
ii) They had to get up
iii) They had to go out
iv) They had to collect

The Lord provided but it was the responsibility of the people to collect. Anyone who didn't respond would miss out on the Lord's provision for that day. The people had to believe the Lord, they had to decide and act and they had to commit time and effort to receiving the fulness of the provision that the Lord had for them.
We go on to read that the Lord told the people through Moses that they were not to store the manna.

> *And Moses said, Let no man leave of it till the morning. Notwithstanding they hearkened not unto Moses; but some of them left of it until the morning, and it bred worms, and stank: and Moses was wroth with them. (Exo 16:19-20)*

There was daily provision for the people of the Lord. Each day the Lord provided a portion for each and every one of His children. This provision could not sustain them into the future though. It was provision for that day, it was their daily bread. In order to satisfy their appetites, the people had to seek out daily their daily bread. Yesterday's provision was not enough to sustain the people for the days ahead. The past provision wouldn't sustain their future needs. They had to daily seek their provision from the Lord.

In John 6 Jesus tells us that He is the true manna that came down from heaven (John 6:32,35). John also tells us that Jesus was the Word made flesh (John 1). Jesus was the embodiment of the Word of God made flesh. It is Jesus as the fulness of the Word that is the spiritual manna upon which the people of the Lord now feast. Each day the Lord has a revelation of His Word to nourish the spiritual appetite of His children through Him who is the Word. Jesus, the Word of God, is the daily portion that we partake of.

There exists a daily provision of the revelation of His Word for His people. Daily we are to seek Him for this, for we cannot live on yesterday's bread. He has fresh revelation for us if we would pray unto Him for it. To do that, like Israel, we need to believe Him for it, decide to act upon it and commit time and effort to collect it. In the writer's mind it is interesting that the natural manna fell with the dew in the morning, but would dissipate as the dew was melted by the

Application

sun. The manna was a priority at the start of the day for the people of the Lord. Such would speak of the need for us to seek the Lord early and feed upon Him before our days begin.

The Lords promise to His people is a provision daily bread. The only reason we have a famine from that is if we are failing to seek it out daily. The spiritual locusts come to distract us and prohibit us from collecting this spiritual manna. The locusts would seek to come and rob us of this provision. They would seek to stop His people from gathering this bread, but it is there daily, and we must of needs avail ourselves of it.

To overcome the spiritual locusts we need to pray to the Father for our daily bread. The locusts seek to starve the people of the Word and rob them of their hope. When His people press into Him in prayer for their daily bread, they overcome the locusts and receive the strengthening of Hope that comes from the truth of His Word.

c) Pray against pestilence
 1) Natural
Pestilence in the natural means death. The opposite of death is life and the Church is to pray natural life into areas that require it. We are to stand against sickness and infirmity and in the name of Jesus speak the restoration of life. The Lord has given us an authority to pray against sickness, we need to have the faith to trust His Word in this.

Throughout the ministry of Jesus, He continually prayed for those who were sick and had infirmities. Jesus says in John 10:10 that He has come that we might have life and have it more abundantly. Jesus constantly restored life to circumstances where pestilence had set in. No greater example can be seen than when He raised Lazarus from the grave. Lazarus had been in the grave for four days and it was the belief in Israel that all life would have left the body by this time. Pestilence had seemingly won. Jesus though comes and restores life, defeating pestilence. He raises Lazarus from the grave, restores His life and demonstrates that the power of God is greater than the power of death.

As Christ's followers we are to pray for the same things Jesus did. We are to pray life into circumstances that have been overrun with pestilence.

 2) Spiritual
Pestilence in the natural leads to death in the natural. Pestilence in the spiritual leads to death in the spiritual. The issue here is spiritual death. As we saw in our exposition on 2 Chronicles 7 the judgements of the Lord are cumulative and

progressive. What starts as spiritual drought leads to spiritual famine and ends in spiritual death.

As believers we are to pray for spiritual life. We are to pray it for our brethren, our Churches, our nations and our world. There is a need for the people of the Lord to seek His outpouring of spiritual life. Pestilence is defeated when life is imparted. As the Church we are to pray for the spiritual life of our local Churches, our regions, our countries and for the body of Christ globally.

When we see pestilence coming in the spiritual we are to take up the call to Ezekiel.

> *So I prophesied as I was commanded: and as I prophesied, there was a noise, and behold a shaking, and the bones came together, bone to his bone. And when I beheld, lo, the sinews and the flesh came up upon them, and the skin covered them above: but there was no breath in them. Then said he unto me, Prophesy unto the wind, prophesy, son of man, and say to the wind, Thus saith the Lord GOD; Come from the four winds, O breath, and breathe upon these slain, that they may live. So I prophesied as he commanded me, and the breath came into them, and they lived, and stood up upon their feet, an exceeding great army. Then he said unto me Son of man, these bones are the whole house of Israel: behold, they say, Our bones are dried, and our hope is lost: we are cut off for our parts. (Eze 37:7-11)*

Life had been taken and hope had been removed. Pestilence was what lay before Ezekiel. But as he obeyed the command of the Lord, he prophesised and sought the Lord for the return of life. As Ezekiel was obedient, the Lord was faithful and he saw life return to the dry bones. Pestilence was overcome when Ezekiel sought the Lord for life That is the call to the Church. When we recognise pestilence we are to speak life and seek the Lord for its restoration.

There lays a responsibility on the people of God, to gather together as the Church, His chosen place, and pray. We are to rise in intercession and seek the Lord with a fervency that would mirror Elijah's. We are to stand in the gap and pray with the same tenaciousness as Abraham had. We pray continually unto the Lord until we see His answers. It takes time and commitment, but it is the call of the Lord to His people. He tells us in His Word that we must needs be seeking Him in prayer for these things. The call for the Church is to be a House of prayer.

4.   Seek His Face

Application

To see the face of Jesus is to have our eyes fixed on Him and ever look to be getting closer to Him. It is the shutting out of other distractions and having Jesus as the priority of focus in our lives.

We see a great example of this when Peter walks on the water. In Matthew 14 we read that after a time of ministry Jesus sends the disciples off in a boat while He goes away to pray by himself. During this time the disciples sailed into midst of the sea and here the ship was being tossed to and fro, as it was being buffeted by contrary winds. As this was happening, in the fourth watch of the night, the disciples suddenly spot Jesus walking on the water. The disciples initially cry out in fear at what they think is a ghost, but Jesus quickly calms them and reassures them that it is Him and that there is nothing to be afraid of. Peter then speaks up and says to Jesus that if it is really Him, tell me to come to you on the water. Jesus responds and tells Peter to simply come. Peter in faith, steps out of the boat and starts walking to Jesus. It is here that we see the focus of Peter. It is the same focus that we need.

Around Peter the winds are blowing, the waves are rolling and the seas are roaring. There are distractions and the circumstances of life happening all around Peter. Peter's priority of focus though is on the Lord. His eyes are fixed upon Jesus and with each step he is seeking to get closer to His face. Peters focus is fixed. Yes the things of the world are happening all around him, but these are all distractions, seeking to rob him of his focus and draw him of his course.

The Church, and the believers who make it, are to follow in the footsteps of Peter. Yes there are things in the world that are happening around us and some of these are extremely important. We have work, we have families, we have commitments and these all require our attention. These are all facts of life. But these should never be the top priority in our lives. We must fix our eyes upon Jesus and prioritise seeking Him. He is our priority of focus. The other things happen but our focus remains on Him.

Wherever our focus is, there our feet will follow. If we are to truly seek His face, the priority of our focus must be on Him. When Peter's focus shifted from Jesus to the waves his feet failed. No matter how hard we try to convince ourselves otherwise, the same will happen to us if our focus isn't fixed on Him. As the people of God we are to prioritise Jesus as the focus of our lives. Jesus should not fit in around the plans and circumstances of life, the plans and circumstances of life should fit around Him. He is to be our priority, He is to be our focus and with each step we take, we are to seek His face. If we can do this and have Him as our focus, the distractions of life will dim and we will find ourselves going on with the Lord as never before. We are to seek His face.

5.   Turn from their wicked ways

Again, it is to be remembered here that this is an address to believers, Christians, as the people of God. More specifically the call is to His people, which collectively are the Church.

In our original definition of wicked ways we noted that: To turn from is to change one's stance. It is to make a one hundred and eighty degree change in direction. We turn from one thing and change our gaze to face another. To turn from a wicked way, is to turn from going towards it and point ourselves in another direction. A wicked way in its simplest form is really anything that is opposite to the commands of God. These are not necessarily massive errors in the lives of His people (though they can be), but can be any path, however minor, that isn't leading towards Him.

It is not the writer's preposition that the Church is full of wicked ways, but rather that the Church, and we as individual believers who make it, need to examine ourselves to see if there are any ways in our lives that may not necessarily be leading to Jesus. It would be unwise to think that there are not areas that need to be looked at. As we noted in our Exposition, 1 Pet 4:17 tells us that judgment must begin with the House of God and Jesus advises in Matthew 4 that we must look at ourselves before judging others.

The Holy Spirit is ever looking to refine His Church to make her ready as the perfect bride of Christ. He is not necessarily looking at extreme errors but rather those small spots that need refining and moulding. He is ever wanting to transform us and He does this as we cooperate, introspect and allow Him to reveal what He is wanting to show us. As Churches and believers who make up the Church, that is the call that rests upon us.

This same call is evidenced in the book of Revelation as Jesus calls unto His Church. In Chapter 1 of Revelation John starts by greeting the seven Churches to whom the epistle was written. Then in Chapters 2 and 3 John goes on to reveal the words of Jesus to these seven Churches. These are the calls of Jesus for the Churches to His the words, introspect and turn from the ways that He was highlighting to them.

It has been said that these seven Churches have a threefold application:

- a) They represent the actual seven Churches of Asia at that time
- b) They are prophetical of the Church through the ages, from Pentecost to the second coming. Each Church represents a era in the life of the Church.
- c) They are prophetical of the seven types of Churches that will exist in the last days.

Our purpose here is not to do a thorough exposition on the letters to the seven Churches, that is a study in itself. What we want to focus on here is that Jesus in each of these letters is addressing the Church, be it actual or prophetical. These letters are to the Church. The Lord is looking on His people, His Church, His chosen place and is given a frank assessment of them. From these seven Churches we see the call of the Lord for them to address the errors that where in them. His constant hope is that they will have an ear to hear what is being said to them and that they will respond to the refining that He is trying to bring. As we look at the letters to these seven Churches we are not looking in judgement but rather looking to highlight the fact that if the Church in John's time, being sixty or so years from its birth in Acts 2, had things that they already needed to turn from how can we as the Church of today think that we may not? With that in mind let us look at what the Lord reveals to His Churches:

a) The Church at Ephesus
The error of lost love (Rev 2:1-7)

The Lord starts by listing all of the positives of the Church at Ephesus. If anyone was to just read verses 2 and 3 of Revelation Chapter 2 they would read a glowing review of the Church. It would be a Church that many would be happy to attend. But the Lord goes onto say:

Nevertheless I have somewhat against thee, because thou hast left thy first love. (Rev 2:4)

The Church was doing well. They had been obedient and persevered through hard times, but they had left their first love. What started as fire and zeal had possibly turned into tradition and repetition. They carried out the functions and actions of a Church, but the love and focus toward God had waned long ago. The Lord comes and commends them for their great qualities, but he then addresses the error that existed. Their love had wearied and it needed to be refired.

The Lord goes onto tell them to remember their first love and repent. They were to examine themselves, recalling what they had been and consider what the Lord was telling them. They were then to repent. To repent literally means to turn. Here they were to return to their first love. They were to turn from their luke-warmness and return to their first love. They were called to turn from the error of luke-warmness.

b) The Church at Pergamos
The error of false doctrine (Rev 2:12-17)

In addressing the Church at Pergamum the Lord points out to them that there is an issue with their doctrine. Their doctrine was not pure as the Lord intended, it was mixed. In the Church was the doctrine of Christ but they also had the doctrine of Balaam and the doctrine of the Nicolaitan's.

The New Testament Church was constantly warned about maintaining the purity of their doctrine. In Peters second epistle he warns that false teachers would come in that would secretly bring in false doctrines. With just a little bit of leaven they would affect the doctrine of the Church. This is what ended up happening at Pergamum. Mixture had been allowed in and it had affected the Churches doctrine. In Deuteronomy 32 the Lord says:

My doctrine shall drop as the rain, my speech shall distil as the dew, as the small rain upon the tender herb, and as the showers upon the grass: (Deu 32:2)

The true doctrine of the Lord has a refreshing quality that rejuvenates a believer's soul and springs forth life. Mixed doctrine robs the believer of this. The Church at Pergamum was missing the refreshing of the Lord because of their mixed doctrine.

In Acts Chapter 2 we are told that the people of Berea were more noble than the Thessalonians, because although they received the words of Paul and Silas readily, they also went and daily searched the scriptures to make sure that the doctrine that was being presented to them lined up with the Word of God. That is what the Church at Pergamum should have done. In these days we as the Church must measure all teaching by the Word of God and not by man's opinion. This will aid us greatly in identifying areas of doctrine that may be not quite right. Pergamum had not done this and the Lord comes to draw their attention to this error in order that it may be dealt with immediately.

c)   The Church at Thyatira
The error of false prophets (Rev 2:18-29)
The previous error addressed false teaching, this error addresses false prophets. The Word tells us that we are to judge a tree by the fruit it produces. It is clear from this passage of Revelation that good fruit was not being produced, yet an individual was allowed to carry on in a self-appointed office corrupting the minds and hearts of believers. This comes back to a governance and leadership issue. One has to question why this was allowed to continue and why no one stood to oppose it. Part of leaderships role is to oversee and protect the flock from potential harm. This had not been done in Thyatira and the Lord was imploring His Church to correct this situation.

d)   The Church at Sardis
The error of self-deception (Rev 3:1-6

The Lord doesn't mince His words here as Sardis is described as the lifeless Church. He knows about their works. He also knows that they are known as being alive, but His verdict is the opposite. He sees Sardis as a dead Church. We see with Sardis the effect of self-deception. Sardis had the appearance of being alive, but on the inside, this was not the case. The outward and the inward didn't match. Sardis from an outside perspective looked like it was full of life. In the natural it looked like the place to be and would have been attractive to those who laid eyes upon it. The spiritual state though was the exact opposite. What looked alive in the natural was dead in the spiritual. Sardis potentially got caught up with the appearance of what they were doing and lost focus on the reason for why they were doing it. God will ever look upon the heart and disregard the outside appearance (1 Sam 16:7). The call to Sardis was to strengthen that which remained.

e) The Church at Laodicea
The error of Luke warmness (Rev 3:14-22)

The Church of Laodicea reads as an apathetic Church that went through the motions of Christianity. They believed they were self sufficient and had little need of the Lord. They believed in the Lord enough to carry on the "traditions" of Christianity but that's about all. The Lord was wanting a relationship with them but to date they hadn't responded to His knocks on the door. Laodicea perceived that they had the ability to meet many of their own needs and as such they lacked a real faith in God. Their reliance on Him and was non-existent. It sounds very much like a congregation of Sunday saints; they would tick off Church on a Sunday, but that is as far as their relationship went. God was calling out to them for more. Just as He did then, Jesus still desires a relationship with His people, not just a once a week visit.

The Lord in addressing the Churches in the book of Revelation reveals a number of errors that existed within them. It is not the writer's heart to speak condemnation or judgement over the Church of today but rather to encourage the Church to have an ear to hear what the Spirit would say. There may be no errors to turn from, as indeed not all of the Churches were revealed to have errors in the book of Revelation, but it would be dangerous grounds if we were not at least open to receiving that possibility from the Lord. Even the faithful Church of Philadelphia was still called by the Lord to have an ear to hear what the Spirit was saying. Throughout each of the seven addresses to the Churches the constant call of the Lord is that the Churches would have an ear to hear what the Spirit is saying.

The call of the Lord in regard to His people turning from their wicked ways is the exact same call. It is to have an ear to hear what the Spirit would say. There may just be some minor errors He wants to highlight in order to take us further and deeper in Him, or there may be nothing, He just wants us to be open to hear what He would say. For the Churches of today it is imperative that we have ears to hear what the Spirit would say and to be ever open to His correction and leading.

> *Search me, O God, and know my heart: try me, and know my thoughts: And see if there be any wicked way in me, and lead me in the way everlasting. (Psa 139:23-24)*

His People are now the Church and the believers that make it up. The "If" responsibilities now lay on us. When the judgements of the Lord are in the earth, be they natural, spiritual or both, then it is up to His people to humble themselves, pray, seek His face and turn from their wicked ways. The Lord is ever after His people to truly press into Him. The onus and responsibility lies upon us as believers. That which was given to Solomon for Israel, was exemplified through Elijah, now rests upon the Church. The Lord's call for us is to press into Him in a greater and more fervent way. He calls us to respond to His Word and to seek Him for relief from spiritual and natural drought, famine and pestilence. If My people who are the Church, called by the name Christians, will humble themselves, pray, seek My face and turn from their wicked ways is the call to the Church today.

D. The Response
Behold, how good and how pleasant it is for brethren to dwell together in unity! ………
for there the LORD commanded the blessing, even life for evermore. (Psa 133:1-3)

When brethren dwell together in unity there I command a blessing says the Lord. But this is not just talking about any type of unity. We are told in Matthew:

> *For where two or three are gathered together in My name, there am I in the midst of them. (Mat 18:20)*

What unites us is the name of the Lord. It is when we are gathered, united in spirit and cause with a focus on the Lord Jesus Christ that the Lord commands a blessing. It is as the Church gathers, forming the chosen place, united as the people of God with a focus on humbling themselves, praying, seeking His face and turning that the Lord commands a blessing:

1. He looks at the drought and provides rain and an outpouring of His Word and Spirit.
2. He looks at locusts and restores provision and an outpouring of understanding, teaching and revelation in His Word, restoring hope.
3. He looks at pestilence and restores life.

When the Church fulfils the "If" requirements the Lord looks at His judgements and brings blessing. He moves in a way that we have not seen and takes His people deeper in relationship with Him. The Lord doesn't just replace judgement with blessing, He outpours His blessing and restores the years that the locusts have eaten.

The Lord is ever faithful and will always act in accordance with His Word. His response is always blessing, but it is our actions that determine whether this is outpoured or not.

Application

E. <u>The Promise</u>

Throughout our Exposition and Example we have seen that the promise of the Lord is that His eyes are open and His ears are attentive to His chosen place. The Church, as the chosen place of the Lord, now has His focus. When we come together as His people, gathering in unity, forming the Church, His eyes are upon us and His ears are attentive unto us. The promise made to Solomon and proven to Elijah rests with the Church. This is the promise that we have as His people. He hears and He sees when we come together as the Church. His eyes are ever upon and His ears are ever attentive to His Church.

If My People

APPLICATON SUMMARY

As we look at the book of Acts in the New Testament we see the application of the truths that were set forth in the Old Testament. As we moved through Acts Chapter 2 we saw the application of what had been revealed to Solomon in 2 Chronicles 7:11-16 and exemplified through Elijah in 1 Kings 18.

A. <u>The Chosen Place</u>

The chosen place of the Lord is now seen to be the Church. The chosen place is no longer a material building, but a spiritual reality. The chosen place is formed as His people come together as the Church, joining in unity and focus. This is the New Testament reality. The Lord showed his acceptance and choice of the Church when His Holy fire fell on the day of Pentecost in the form of tongues upon the disciples gathered together. Here, when the one hundred and twenty where gathered together in unity, in the name of the Lord, the birth of the Church occurred as we know it. It is the Holy accepting fire of the Lord that shows His choice. The chosen place is now the Church.

Just as we see in our Exposition and Example the chosen place is interwoven with prayer and sacrifice. The Church, as the New Testament chosen place of the Lord, is to be a place of prayer and a place where believers present themselves as living sacrifices unto the Lord.

B. <u>The Judgements</u>

The truths of the judgements of the Lord carry through to the Church. The judgements of no rain, locusts and pestilence remain the same. But we considered here the application of the natural and the spiritual judgements of the Lord. It is first the natural and then the spiritual.

1. No rain
   a) Natural drought.
   b) Spiritual drought of the Spirit and the Word.
2. Locusts
   a) Natural lack of provision, oppression.
   b) Spiritual lack of provision of the Word of God, spiritual life oppressed.
2. Pestilence
   a) Natural death – a result of drought and famine.
   b) Spiritual death – a result of spiritual drought and spiritual famine.

As with the natural so with the spiritual. The judgements are progressive and each is intended to try and capture the attention of His people and cause them to turn back to Him

Application Summary

C. The People

The people referred to here are the people of the Lord, His children. It is those that are called by His name. The call is to us as believers who collectively make up the Church. The chosen place and my people are really one and the same thing in the New Testament application. It is His people gathered together that make the Church and it is the Church unto whom the call goes out to.

The Lord in the book of Acts takes the Old Testament truths and, through His revelation of the Church as the chosen place, applies these truths to the believers who make up the Church. It is upon we believers as the Church that the "If" responsibilities now lie. "If" we as His people will respond, "Then" He will come in mercy. The expectation and onus is now upon us:

1. If we His people - Christians who form the Church
2. Will humble ourselves – as children
3. And pray – as Elijah
4. And seek His face – as Peter
5. And turn from our wicked ways – being attentive and having an ear to hear what the Spirit would say

It is up to us as His people to respond in the ways the Lord has outlined if we want to see Him respond to the natural and spiritual judgements that are in our lands.

D. The Response

As we as believers gather together (the Church, the Chosen place) in unity (in His name) there He commands a blessing (Ps 133). As we do this and fulfil the "If" conditions of the previous section, His promise to us is that:

1. He will hear – He hears our fervent prayers and intercessions.
2. He will forgive – He forgives our wrong ways when we repent.
3. He will heal – He provides blessing and restores the years the locust has eaten.

The Lord is ever faithful, but His response is determined by the actions of His people. If we return to Him, He turns the judgments into blessings.

E. The Promise

The eyes and ears of the Lord are ever attentive to His chosen place, the Church. This is not a natural building, but a spiritual gathering of His people united in His name. When the people of God come together to form the Church He sees and hears the actions and cries of His people. His focus is upon His Church.

If My People

SUMMARY OF EXPOSITION, EXAMPLE AND APPLICATION

During this study we have moved through Exposition to Example and finally to Application. As we have done this, we have hopefully seen the same truths of the Lord revealed and applied. Our purpose here is to surmise those truths and hopefully re-enforce in the mind of the reader how these apply to the Church. What was revealed and exemplified in the natural is applied spiritually to the Church. It is the writer's sincere belief that if we as believers can see what God has revealed in His Word, then our Churches are going to go deeper in God and see Him move in powerful ways.

A. <u>The Chosen Place</u>

We started this study with our exposition of 2 Chronicles 7 where we looked at the truths that the Lord was revealing and focused on five main points. We then moved to 1 Kings 18 where we saw the truths of 2 Chronicles 7 in a practical example through the account of Elijah and the prophets of Baal on Mount Carmel. Finally, we got to the book of Acts and the birth of the Church. Here we saw that the Lord has shown His Church to be His New Testament chosen place. The fire of the Lord once again fell, this time consuming each of the one hundred and twenty gathered with the power and presence of the Holy Spirit. It was again the fire of the Lord that declared His chosen place and highlighted this as the place where New Testament believers are to come together, pray and present themselves as living sacrifices unto the Lord. There is power when we individually pray, but when we come together in unity, forming the Church, in obedience to the Word of God and seek Him, presenting ourselves as living sacrifices, we go to another level.

2 Chronicles 7	**1 Kings 18**	**Acts 2**
Temple of Solomon	Mount Carmel	The Upper Room
Great Gathering – dedication of the temple	Great Gathering – All Israel assembled	Great gathering – Feast of Pentecost
Solomon	Elijah	The one hundred and twenty.
Offering and Sacrifice	Offering and Sacrifice	Living sacrifices
Glory filled the House		Upper Room Filled
Fire of the Lord	Fire of the Lord	Fire of the Lord
Fire descended	Fire descended	Fire descended
Consumed the offerings and sacrifices	Consumed the offerings, sacrifice, water, altar and dust.	Consumed the living sacrifice – the disciples filled
Natural House	Natural Mountain	Spiritual House
The Temple of Solomon – The House of God		The Church – the House of God
The Chosen Place	The Chosen Place	The Chosen Place

Summary of Exposition, Example and Application

The Place of Heard Prayer	The Place of Heard Prayer	The Place of Heard Prayer
The Place of Sacrifice	The Place of Sacrifice	The Place of Living Sacrifices

B. <u>The Judgements</u>

In 2 Chronicles the Lord outline three judgements that will affect His people. These were the judgements of a shut heaven, locusts and pestilence. When we came to 1 Kings, we saw these judgements occurring in the nation of Israel as the people had turned their backs on the Lord. Having seen and looked at the natural aspects of these we then moved to consider their spiritual application to the New Testament believer as we considered Acts 2.

2 Chronicles 7	**1 Kings 18**	**Acts 2**	**Effects**
Natural	Natural	Natural and Spiritual	
Shut up heaven that there be no rain – drought	The rains were shut up for three and a half years – Israel was in drought	Natural drought. Spiritual drought of the Spirit and the Word	Effects life and the ability of life to be produced
If I command locusts to devour the land – lack of provision	The land was in famine – lack of provision, oppression	Natural famine Spiritual famine of the provision of the Word as our daily bread, spiritual oppression	Effects hope
Or if I send pestilence	Loss of livestock	Natural death Spiritual death	Takes life and hope

As with the natural so with the spiritual, the judgements are progressive and the end result is death be it natural or spiritual. The judgements of the Lord are ever to get the attention of His people and seek to turn them back to Him. His judgements only progress if His people fail to hear what He is saying.

C. <u>The People</u>

In 2 Chronicles the call of My people was the nation of Israel. In 2 Kings, whilst the nation of Israel had been split into two Kingdom, the call of My people still went to the natural children of Abraham. It was to Elijah and the people of the kingdom of Israel that the call was too. In Acts though, we saw how this call changed. The call that was once to natural Israel now rests with spiritual Israel. In the New Testament "My people" are believers who have accepted the Lord Jesus Christ as their saviour and been baptised into His name. It is to us as Christians to whom this applies. The responsibilities to fulfil the "If" statement of 2 Chronicles rest upon us. It is upon His people gathering together as the Church (the chosen place) that the onus lies.

2 Chronicles 7	1 Kings 18	Acts 2
My people – the children of God, the united houses of Israel and Judah	My People – Elijah and the nation of Israel	Christians united in the name of Jesus
Will Humble themselves	Elijah falls before the Lord The people fall on their faces	Need to humble ourselves
Pray	Elijah prayed repeatedly for the Lord to intercede	Need to pray for the natural and spiritual judgements
Seek my face	Elijah sought the face of the Lord	Need to seek the face of the Lord as our priority
Turn from their wicked ways	The people turned from their idol worship and divided hearts	Need to turn from those errors that the Lord would reveal to His Church by His Spirit

D. The Response

As with the previous points, we again see that the response of the Lord flows through the three sections we have looked at in this study. His response is constant and ever dependant upon the actions of His people. If they will seek Him, He will respond. He tells is in 2 Chronicles 7 what His response will be, He proves His Word in 2 Kings and it is the truth of this promise that now rests with the Church.

2 Chronicles 7	1 Kings 18	Acts 2
I will hear from heaven	The Lord heard the prayer of Elijah	The Lord will hear
I will forgive their sin	He forgave the sins of the people when they humbled themselves before Him	The Lord will forgive
I will heal their land	He sends rain to heal the land	The Lord will heal

E. The Promise

The promise of the Lord remains the same for His people throughout the examples we have considered. His Promise is unfailing and unwavering. His eyes and ears are ever upon His chosen place. Whilst the place of the Lord may have changed, the promise never faulters. We see from the scriptures that we considered that:

2 Chronicles 7	1 Kings 18	Acts 2
My eyes will be upon the Temple of Solomon	The Lord's eyes were on Mount Carmel	His eyes are upon His Church
My ears are attentive to The Temple of Solomon	The Lord's ears were attentive to Mount Carmel	His ears are attentive to His Church
The promise of the Lord spoken	The promise fulfilled	The promise to be fully realised

CONCLUSION

Through Part A of this study we have seen that what we learnt in 2 Chronicles 7 and all that we saw exemplified in 1 Kings 18 now applies to the Church. In Acts Chapter 2 when the Lord sent the tongues of fire down upon the disciples who were gathered together and filled the upper room with the wind of His Spirit He was fulfilling the truths He had set forth with the Temple of Solomon. The Lord shows to us that it is the Church, believers gathered together in unity, that are now His chosen place. What was once signified by a natural, material temple is now fulfilled in a spiritual gathering. It is His people, joining together in His name that the Lord declares to be His chosen place.

The Church as the chosen place is to be a place of prayer and spiritual sacrifice where we present ourselves unto the Lord. It is to be a place where His people press into Him with a fervency and tenacity seeking His will be done on earth as it is in Heaven.

Once we understand the Church to be the chosen place we then understand that the responsibility of action in regards to the judgements of the Lord in the earth, be they natural or spiritual, lies with us, Christians, who corporately and collectively make up the Church. The Church is the chosen place and it is upon those that make up the Church that the onus now lies. That which once rested on the shoulders of natural Israel now rests on the shoulders of spiritual Israel.

For the people of the Lord to walk in the fulness of the blessings that He has for us we need to grab hold of this message. The Lord desires for His people to walk in His blessings. The responsibility lies with us though. We determine, through our actions, what we walk in. The call of the Lord is for His people to return to His blessings.

WHEN the judgements of a shut heaven, locusts and pestilence, be they natural or spiritual, are evident,

IF
Those that have accepted Christ and are called by His name
Will humble themselves
And pray
And seek His face
And turn from their wicked ways
At the chosen place, the Church

THEN
The Lord will hear
The Lord will forgive
And the Lord will heal

Conclusion

FOR
His eyes and His ears are ever upon His Chosen Place, which is now the Church.

That which was revealed in 2 Chronicles and exemplified in 1 Kings now applies to the Church. The call of "If My People" now rests upon us as believers. The promised blessings of the Lord are available for His people to walk in, natural and spiritual, if we would heed His call unto us.

If My People

THE CALL TO THE CHURCH

In compiling this study the Lord has constantly stirred the heart of the writer and emphasised to him the importance of the Church realising that we are now the chosen place. It is the importance of understanding the interwovenness of prayer and sacrifice with the chosen place and taking on the responsibilities that come with that. It has been through meditating upon this that the writer has felt the Lord speak a call to the Church. This in a sense is the climax of what this study has led to. The Lord has revealed and applied the truth of His Word, before specifically given a call to the Church of today. It is the writer's sincere hope that the following makes sense and that the reader's heart is stirred just as the writer's has been and continues to be by the Lord.

In 1 Ki 18:41 after the Lord displayed His Holy fire descending from heaven, but before Elijah has gone up the mount to pray, Elijah addresses King Ahab. Elijah speaks to the King and says:

> *And Elijah said unto Ahab, Get thee up, eat and drink; for there is a sound of abundance of rain. (1Ki 18:41)*

After three and a half years of drought the Lord declares through Elijah that there could be heard the sound of the abundance of rain. There was the sound of the abundance of rain. From going over this account it would seem that there was not even a cloud in the sky when Elijah spoke this forth (Elijah didn't stop interceding for the nation until he saw the smallest cloud appear in the sky). There was nothing in the natural and yet Elijah in faith speaks forth this Word of the Lord regarding the sound of rain.

The Hebrew word for abundance here is the word 'Hamon' and means a *noise, tumult, crowd*; also *disquietude, wealth.* These are no occasional sprinkles or showers of rain. These are a rich outpouring of the Lord. This was the sound of a wealth of rain.

Before there is any evidence of showers. Before Elijah seeks the Lord for the rain, he declares by the Word of the Lord that there was the sound of the abundance of rain.

The Lord would declare to His Church the exact same message, that there is the sound of the abundance of rain. There exists for the Church a wealth of spiritual rain to be outpoured. The rains of the Church in these last days are to be a combination of the former and latter. This is not just the former, nor just the latter rains, but both together. There is an abundance of rain to pour out and the Lord would declare that it's sound is there to be heard. Just like with Elijah, the provision already exists. When the Lord spoke through Elijah He said there is the sound of the abundance of rain. He did not say there will be in the future. He said there existed now the sound of the abundance of rain. He would say the same to the Church in these days.

With that word though comes a responsibility. A responsibility now lies on us, Christians, spiritual Israel to seek the Lord at the chosen place. Elijah declared the sound of the abundance and then he went up the mount of God to seek the Lord. Elijah declared in faith and then went to the place that God had shown to be His chosen place to pray and intercede. The question that struck the writer's mind is would the rains have still come if he had stopped at simply declaring the sound? Would the Lord still have sent the rains if Elijah had spoken about the sound of the abundance, but then simply returned home? The answer is No. The rains came because although Elijah spoke in faith he then acted in accordance with the Word of God revealed in 2 Chronicles and sought the Lord at His chosen place. It was through humbling himself, seeking the Lords face, praying and turning that Elijah saw the fulfillment of the sound of the abundance of rain. Why would/should we expect things to be different in our situation?

There is an onus and responsibility that lies upon the Church to see the fulfillment of the rains. We have the onus to humble ourselves, to pray, to seek His face and turn and we are not to just do this once, but like Elijah persist until we see the fulfillment of what has been promised. Seven times it says that Elijah returned and sought the Lord until he saw the answer of the Lord. The Church as the chosen place is to press in and seek the Lord with a passion and fervency. The Lord is looking for a tenaciousness in His people to continue seeking Him until we see the fulfillment of His promise.

We see a great example of what is required in 2 Kings 13. As Elisha was on his death bed, King Joash came and visited him. Elisha tells Joash to take up a bow and arrow and fire the arrow out of the window. As Joash does Elisha declares that it symbolised the arrow of the Lord's deliverance from Syria. Elisha then instructed Joash to gather the remaining arrows and strike the ground. Joash did as Elisha said but only stuck the ground three times and was subsequently rebuked by the prophet. The words of Elisha were that Joash would only see partial deliverance for the nation. If he had persisted, he would have seen complete deliverance for the nation (2 Kings 13:14-19). Much like with the example of Elijah and King Ahab, the prophetic word had been spoken forth regarding deliverance, but after this perseverance was required in the actions of Joash. Joash didn't persevere as Elijah did, he gave up after three strikes. His lacked fervency and desperation for the Lord to move.

The Lord is calling His people to a deeper, more fervent lifestyle of seeking Him in His House. He is calling His Church to persist like the widow before the unjust judge (Luke 18:6). He would call us to continually persist until we see Him move. Like Elijah He is calling us to take hold in faith of His Word regarding the abundance of rain and persist until we see that cloud appear on the horizon.

The sound of the rain is there, the Lord has declared that in His Word, but the realisation of these rains comes when His people fulfil the "If" of 2 Chronicles 7. We can sing about the rains, we can speak about the rains, we can write books about the rains. None of these are bad things, but if this is all we do we will not see the fulfillment. It was never going to be enough for Elijah to just prophesy of the rains. If we truly want to see the rains of the Lord poured out then we as His people must come together as the Church, wherever we are, and seek Him according to His Word. The declaration is there. The promise is there. The onus is with us.

Just as the judgements of the Lord are progressive, we see that so too are His blessings. Spiritual drought leads to spiritual famine which results in spiritual death, but spiritual rain leads to spiritual harvest and results in spiritual life. Rain prevents famine and staves off pestilence. The spiritual rain of the Lord, the outpouring of His Spirit and Word, brings revival. Just as the natural is revived when rain comes after periods of drought, so too is it with the spiritual. The spiritual rains of the Lord bring refreshing and revival to His people. That is the promise that rests on the people of God if they will press into Him. What starts with rain will see revival spring forth.

But the rain is ever a result of His people spending time on their knees. It is a result of His people pressing in, going deeper and making Him the priority. It is the result of His people presenting themselves as a living sacrifice in the service of the Lord. As we His people understand the linkage of the chosen place, prayer and sacrifice we will see the Lord move in new and powerful ways.

Revival is a fruit that is produced. Before a tree can ever bear fruit it must of necessity spend time and energy in growing. A tree needs to send down roots so that it is able to hold the fruit it produces. The same is true for the Church. There has to be a solidness and security in our foundations for the Church to be able to hold the fruits of revival that are produced.

Any believer would raise their hand when asked if they want to see revival come. So often we long for the fruits of revival, but like anything revival starts with a seed. True revival always starts with the people of God pressing into Him with fervency, hunger and persistence. The Lord is looking for a renewed hunger and thirst in His people to press in and persist to see the promised rains of the Holy Spirit.

There is the sound of the abundance of rain. The promise of the Lord is there, and the Lord will ever act in response to the actions of His people. The question for the Church is do we hear the sound and will we persist in seeking Him until we see the cloud? The realisation of the rains takes faith, persistence, time and effort. If we can commit to that then there will be an amazing outpouring upon His Church. That is the promised response of the Lord.

If the Church, and the believers who form it, can fulfil the "If" conditions, then we will return to the fulness of His blessings.

PART B: REMAINING IN BLESSING

If My People

SECTION INTRODUCTION

Throughout this study we have looked at the responsibilities that lie with the people of the Lord when His judgements are upon the earth, be they natural or spiritual. Everything that we have seen has been from a response perspective. All that we that we have looked at through the study so far has been to identify what the chosen place is, who the people of God are and what they are to do when His judgements are upon the earth. As we have gone through this, we have seen that once His people fulfil the "If" statement conditions then God will hear, forgive and heal. When His people seek Him the judgements of drought, locusts and pestilence are replaced with the blessings of rain, harvest and life. Blessing replaces judgement. This is true for both the natural and spiritual applications of the judgments and blessings we looked at.

In the writer's mind the question that arose is that after we respond to the judgements of the Lord and return to His blessing, how do we ensure that His judgements are not repeated? Surely once we are walking in the blessing of the Lord that would be a season that we would want to continue in. The one thing that we learn from history though is that we never learn from history. This can be seen throughout the history of Israel in the Old Testament as the nation constantly bounced between the blessings and judgements of the Lord. Mankind has a habit of going around the mountain and repeating the same mistakes. The heart of the writer is to see the Church not only walk in the fulness of what the Lord has for them, but to continue in it. It is to see the Church go from strength to strength and to see the next generation go further than the current. It is to see the people of the Lord enter the fulness of the promises that the Lord has for them.

The purpose of this section is to look at what the Word of God tells us about how we can remain in the blessings of God. We have already considered how we return to the blessings of the Lord, now we will consider how His people can stay there.

CONTINUATION

How to avoid the judgments of the Lord and remain in His blessings.

In looking at how to avoid the recurrence of the judgements of the Lord the writer was directed to Deuteronomy 11:13-21. Here the Lord addresses the same judgements we have looked at throughout this study so far and reveals to His people how to avoid them. The book of Deuteronomy starts off as the people of Israel are about to enter the promised land of the Lord after forty years of wilderness wonderings. The people have been living in obedience unto the Lord and are about to continue in His blessings as they enter the long awaited for land. The Lord in this passage sets before the people a blessing and a curse He literally spelled out for the people of Israel what they needed to do to ensure that they stayed within His blessing. The people had been walking in the favour and blessing of the Lord and as Moses recounts their wilderness wonderings, he implores the people to continue to walk in such a way. For us as the Church this answers the question that arose in the writer's mind in regard to remaining in the blessings of the Lord. It is in this passage that the Church can learn what we are to do when we have seen the Lord respond in blessing to His people seeking Him. It tells us how to remain in His blessing and avoid His judgments. The reader is encouraged to read the below quote from Deuteronomy several of times, before moving ahead with this section.

> *And it shall come to pass, if ye shall hearken diligently unto my commandments which I command you this day, to love the LORD your God, and to serve him with all your heart and with all your soul, That I will give you the rain of your land in his due season, the first rain and the latter rain, that thou mayest gather in thy corn, and thy wine, and thine oil. And I will send grass in thy fields for thy cattle, that thou mayest eat and be full. Take heed to yourselves, that your heart be not deceived, and ye turn aside, and serve other gods, and worship them; And then the LORD'S wrath be kindled against you, and he shut up the heaven, that there be no rain, and that the land yield not her fruit; and lest ye perish quickly from off the good land which the LORD giveth you. Therefore shall ye lay up these my words in your heart and in your soul, and bind them for a sign upon your hand, that they may be as frontlets between your eyes. And ye shall teach them your children, speaking of them when thou sittest in thine house, and when thou walkest by the way, when thou liest down, and when thou risest up. And thou shalt write them upon the door posts of thine house, and upon thy gates: That your days may be multiplied, and the days of your children, in the land which the LORD sware unto your fathers to give them, as the days of heaven upon the earth. (Deu 11:13-21)*

Continuation

For the purpose of this section we will break the above passage from Deuteronomy into three sections and see what truth the Lord would reveal to us. As we move through these sections we will slowly go through each verse, making observations as we go before surmising our thoughts at the end.

A. The Promise of Continued Blessing
And it shall come to pass, if ye shall hearken diligently unto my commandments which I command you this day, to love the LORD your God, and to serve him with all your heart and with all your soul, (Deu 11:13)

We see here from the Lord another "If" statement. He lays out the conditions for His people to remain in His blessing. This "If" statement of the Lord addresses a few areas for the people. The Lord says that "If" they were to obey His commandments, love the Lord and serve Him then they would continue in His blessings. A chapter earlier In Deuteronomy 10 we read a very similar statement from the Lord through Moses. There the Lord says:

> *And now, Israel, what doth the LORD thy God require of thee, but to fear the LORD thy God, to walk in all his ways, and to love him, and to serve the LORD thy God with all thy heart and with all thy soul, To keep the commandments of the LORD, and His statutes, which I command thee this day for thy good? (Deu 10:12-13)*

Here the Lord mentions the same things as in Deuteronomy 11:13 but adds a couple of extra points for us to consider. The Lord would require us to fear Him, walk in His ways, love Him, serve Him and obey Him. If we compare the two passages we see:

Deuteronomy 10:12,13	Deuteronomy 11:13
The Lord requires of you	If you hearken diligently to
Fear Him	
Walk in His ways	
Love Him	Love Him
Serve Him	Serve Him
Obey Him	Obey Him

We see from these two passages that the Lord outlines five cores of obedience for His people. We are told that the "Lord requires" this of us and that we are to "hearken diligently" to these things. The Lord places a great emphasis on these five things', and we see with them the essence of the lives that the people of God are to live. Let us consider them a little deeper.

1. Fear Him
but to fear the LORD thy God

What does it mean to fear the Lord? The topic of fearing the Lord is a study in itself, which is not the purpose of this particular book. For this reason, we will just provide a summary of what Godly fear is.

Throughout scripture we can see that there are two types of fear of the Lord revealed. There is:
- a) An unholy fear based solely on the possibilities of the judgment of God. This is a trembling fear of what God might do to us.
- b) A Holy fear based on the absolute awesomeness of who God is. This is a fear based in reverence of who the Lord is.

The Lord would require that His people would walk in a Holy fear. It is the second definition that is in focus here. True Godly fear is a reverential awe of and for the Most High God. The Hebrew word used in this passage in Deuteronomy means "to fear, morally to revere, causatively to frighten". Godly fear is a reverence for the fulness of who God is.

A proper and true fear of the Lord can be described as:
- a) Allegiance to God based on reverence of and for God.
- b) A fear based on what He has done for us, not what He can do to us.
- c) A fear based in the security of His Love.
- d) A fear based in submission not subjection.
- e) A fear based in reverence, honour and respect.

To fear the Lord is to have a reverence for who He is. In scripture we are told that the fear of the Lord is the beginning of wisdom (Ps 111:10, Pro 9:10). To fear the Lord is to have a clear understanding of who God is, what He has done and what He is yet to do. It is to hold Him in the highest revere.

What does the Lord require of us? To have a reverential respect for who He is i.e. a Godly fear.

2.   Walk in His Ways
to walk in all his ways

To walk implies an action. To walk in His ways implies a way of life. In scripture only two men are recorded as having walked with God, these being Enoch and Noah (Gen 5:22, Gen 6:9). Both of these individuals were men of God whose lives reflected what they believed and whose actions spoke volumes to those who were around them.

To walk in His ways is to walk as He walks. It is to follow in His footsteps. Our lives are a living testimony of what we believe. The way we live our lives preaches Jesus to the world.

Continuation

3. Love Him
and to love him,

The call to hearken diligently is a call to preserve love. Above all else our faith must abound with the essence of love (1 Cor 13:1). He is to be the centre of our love. We are to love Him because He first loved us.

4. Serve Him
and to serve the LORD thy God with all thy heart and with all thy soul,

To serve the Lord is to have Him as the priority of our lives. This is not talking about a people being enslaved to Him, but rather a people who have God as the centre of their lives.

In Matthew 6:24 Jesus says:

> *No man can serve two masters: for either he will hate the one, and love the other; or else he will hold to the one, and despise the other. Ye cannot serve God and mammon. (Mat 6:24)*

The context of this is that no one can have two number one priorities in their lives. There is always going to be one that pushes the other to the side. The same is true of us. If the Lord isn't the number one priority of our lives then something else is and whatever is that number one priority is going to attract our time, attention and focus. For the people of God, He is to be our only number one priority.

5. Obey Him
To keep the commandments of the LORD, and his statutes

We are to obey His commandments. We are to keep His commandments. We are to hearken diligently unto His commandments

In Deuteronomy Chapter 10 Moses recounts how he had to go up the mount of God to get the second set of the ten commandments. The original set had been broken when Moses had descended from the mount and found the people of Israel worshipping the golden calf that Aaron had made at the petitioning of the people of Israel. These ten commandments were written on two tables of stone by the finger of God. These were known as the moral law and could be separated into two groups: commandments towards God and commandments towards men:

Commandments towards God	Commandments towards Men
No other Gods before Him	Honour thy father and mother
No idols	Thou shall not kill

Don't take the Lord's name in vain	Thou shall not commit adultery
Remember the Sabbath and keep it Holy	Thou shall not steal
	Thou shall not bear false witness
	Thou shall not covet

When Jesus was ministering upon the earth He simplified these down to two commandments as detailed in Matt 22:37-39:

Towards God	Towards Men
Thou shall love the Lord with all thy heart, all thy soul and all thy strength	Thou shalt love thy neighbour as thyself

Jesus goes on to say that on these two commandments hang all the law and the prophets (Matt 22:40)

The ten commandments reveal to us the Moral law of God, how man is to live. Jesus takes these ten commandments, condenses them to two commandments but iterates the necessity of the motive behind them. Our obedience is to be based in love. The Lord is not looking for mindless obedience, He is looking for obedience that is born out of a love that goes down to our heart and soul. It is a love not only for the Lord but also unto our neighbours.

True love is at the foundation of our faith. It is out of that true love for God that we can truly love our neighbour. It is through love we fulfil the law. Jesus said that He did not come to abolish the law but fulfil it. He did this with the greatest showing of love that the world has ever seen. To obey His commandments is not only to love God but also to love our fellow man. To obey is to love. We keep His commandments when we love God and love our neighbour. It takes both.

In our study we saw that the Lord required of His people to: humble themselves; pray; seek His face; and turn from their wicked ways. When His people did this, they found themselves returned to a right relationship with the Lord. It is in this time of right fellowship that we naturally fulfil the five cores of obedience as outlined above. When we are in a right relationship with the Lord our lives are in spiritual alignment and we are walking as the Lord would have us to.

That I will give you the rain of your land in his due season, the first rain and the latter rain, that thou mayest gather in thy corn, and thy wine, and thine oil. And I will send grass in thy fields for thy cattle, that thou mayest eat and be full. (Deu 11:14-15)

Continuation

The Lord outlines the call to His people to continue in obedience and He then goes on to explain the blessings of the Lord that follow this. There would be the blessing of rain, harvest and life. These are the same blessings of the Lord that we discovered in our Part A of this study. There we saw that there was both a natural and a spiritual application to the blessings of God for His people. The natural explanation is self-explanatory here so we will not spend time expounding this again. We will though quickly recap the spiritual application of these blessings to prompt our memory:

1. They would have rain in its due season.
That I will give you the rain of your land in his due season, the first rain and the latter rain

There would be the early rains and the latter rains. There would be no drought. Spiritually it points to a pouring out of His Word and His Spirit.

2. There would be harvest.
thou mayest gather in thy corn, and thy wine, and thine oil

There would be the harvest of the corn, the wine and the oil. It is a threefold harvest and speaks of plenty of provision in the natural. Spiritually it points to a harvest of man's understanding and revelation in the Word. It is a harvest of scriptural truths for spiritual man. There is spiritual blessing, growth, freedom and life.

3. Life would be sustained through the provision that the Lord would provide.
And I will send grass in thy fields for thy cattle, that thou mayest eat and be full

This part of the verse stands in stark contrast to King Ahab's situation in 1 Kings 18. There pestilence reigned as there was no grass in the fields for the cattle to be sustained under the judgment of the Lord. Here there is an abundance of provision allowing life to thrive.

1 Kings 18	Deuteronomy 11
Judgement of the Lord	Blessing of the Lord
…….. peradventure we may find grass to save the horses and mules alive, that we lose not all the beasts. (1Ki 18:5)	*And I will send grass in thy fields for thy cattle, that thou mayest eat and be full.(Deu 11:15)*
Lack	Abundance
Pestilence	Life

The abundance of the Lord here blesses man with life. The spiritual state of man thrives and is nourished in the blessings of the Lord. We see spiritual life flourishing as a result of the rains and the harvest.

The blessings of rain, harvest and life are the same blessings that we have discovered throughout our study so far. These blessings are not only a response from the Lord to His people returning and seeking Him afresh, but the blessings continue as His people diligently hearken unto the Lord and His commandments in love. The blessings exist not only for those that return to the Lord, but also for those who continue in Him. When His people return and continue to live in the manner of their return the blessings of the Lord flow. As His people walk with Him the blessings of rain, harvest and life continue. It is to be remembered from our earlier sections that these blessings have both a natural and a spiritual application to the people of God and the Church. The reader is referred back to the previous sections for an overview of these blessings.

As we continue to walk with the Lord, the promise of the Lord is to maintain His blessings for us. The question remains, how do we do that? How do we continue in obedience?

B. <u>The warning of judgement</u>
Take heed to yourselves, that your heart be not deceived, and ye turn aside, and serve other gods, and worship them; (Deu 11:16)

The language changes here as the Lord issues a warning to His people. He instructs them to take heed. The Hebrew word for take heed in this verse means to hedge about, guard, to protect, to attend to. It carries the thought of needing to be on watch for one's own self-preservation. The Lord's Word to His people is that they needed to guard themselves.

It is interesting that the Lord has just outlined what He requires of His people, informs them of the blessings that will follow and then tells them to take heed. Why is that? The Lord addresses His people, because as the history of the Bible shows us, when the people of the Lord live in blessing they tend to take their eyes off the Lord and become complacent. The call of the Lord here is to take heed that in blessing you do not become complacent.

For the Church the history of natural Israel can be prophetic of the experiences of spiritual Israel. The same call of the Lord rests upon us. Whether we are in the natural blessings of the Lord or the spiritual we need to take heed. For the Church this message to take heed is really the first step in ensuring that we continue in the blessing of God. Having sought the Lord to see His blessings replace His judgements we must make sure that we take heed. We cannot afford to become complacent, let our guard down or fail to attend to.

The Lord then goes on to list the process of decline that His people will go through if they fail to take heed. If we fail to guard ourselves, attend to ourselves, protect ourselves then we leave ourselves open. When we fail to take heed we open the door for spiritual decline. The Lord outlines four steps of spiritual decline that occur in this verse from Deuteronomy 11:

Continuation

1. Hearts deceived
that your heart be not deceived,

Take heed that your hearts be not deceived. This warning gives the clear implication that our hearts have the capability of being deceived. They are not steadfast but are open to the possibility of deception. In this statement there are two parts for us to consider:

a) What is deception

Deception in its simplest form is believing a lie as truth. Deception seeks to either hide the truth or present a lie as truth. In either case to be deceived is to believe in something that is not completely and utterly true.

In Genesis 27 we see a great example of how deception works. Here we read that Isaac, the father of Esau and Jacob, was well advanced in years. His eyes were dim and he believed the day of his death would be soon approaching. In light of this he calls his eldest son and firstborn, Esau, and asks him to go hunting and prepare him some savoury food after which Isaac would pronounce the blessing of the firstborn upon him. Rebekah, Isaac's wife, overheard this and called Jacob, the second born son, but her favourite. Rebekah tells Jacob to go to the flock and fetch two choice kids. She would prepare them for Isaac and would help Jacob deceive his father into thinking he was Esau. The plan was that Jacob would receive the blessing of the firstborn instead of Esau.

Rachel prepared the food and then had Jacob dress in the best clothes of Esau. Finally, she put the skins of the goats on the smooth parts of Jacobs hands and neck to mimic the hairiness of Esau. Isaac's eyes were dim and his vision impaired, so this deception involved tricking the other senses of Isaac. Our senses are what communicate information to our brain and in order for us to be deceived, deception has to come through one of these gates. There are five gates through which deception can enter.

1) Eye gate
And it came to pass, that when Isaac was old, and his eyes were dim, so that he could not see, (Gen 27:1)

The old saying is never judge a book by its cover, yet so often we make a judgement based solely on what we see. Isaac couldn't see properly, his eyes were dim, which made it easier for Jacob to deceive him through his appearance.

2) Ear gate
The voice is Jacob's voice, but the hands are the hands of Esau. (Gen 27:22)

Jacob tried to deceive his father through his words. He claimed to be Esau and lied about the food he had prepared. Isaac's ears though detected the lie. He recognised the voice of Jacob and had doubts about what was being said to him.

3) Nose gate

And he came near, and kissed him: and he smelled the smell of his raiment, and blessed him, and said, See, the smell of my son is as the smell of a field which the LORD hath blessed: (Gen 27:27)

Jacob wore Esau's clothes which caused him to smell like his brother. This added to the deception that Isaac was experiencing. The odours deceived his sense of smell.

4) Touch gate

And he discerned him not, because his hands were hairy, as his brother Esau's hands: so he blessed him. (Gen 27:23)

The hands are of Esau. The skins of the goats deceived Isaac. His sense of touch was deceived. The Word says that "he discerned him not for his hands were hairy".

5) Taste gate

And he said, Bring it near to me, and I will eat of my son's venison, that my soul may bless thee. And he brought it near to him, and he did eat: and he brought him wine, and he drank. (Gen 27:25)

The meal tasted like something that Esau would have made. Esau was out hunting venison, but Rebekah had told Jacob to fetch two kids of the goats from the flock. Rebekah had done such a good job of impersonating Esau's cooking that Jacob couldn't taste the difference between venison and goat.

How did Jacob deceive his father? He presented a lie as the truth. He presented himself as his brother. Isaac's doubts were put aside because of the persuasiveness of the lie. Isaac was taken in by the lie that was presented to him. His senses were deceived and he couldn't deny the information that was coming in. He suspected deception but was eventually overcome by how compelling the lie was.

Deception prays on our weaknesses and seeks to overcome our senses. Deception dresses a lie as truth and seeks to lodge it in our minds. Deception targets the mind and seeks to overcome our thoughts through deceiving our senses.

b) How is the heart deceived?

Continuation

The heart is deceived when those deceptive thoughts move from our head to our heart. Deception enters though the senses, seeking to infiltrate our minds and move to our hearts. It is a three-fold process:

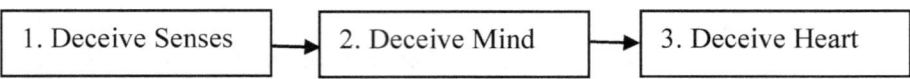

It is for this reason we are told to take captive every thought and make it obedient to Christ. If we can take care of the thought before it moves any further, then we protect our hearts. What starts in the mind takes root in the heart if we dwell upon it.

The reason that we are to take heed that our hearts be not deceived is that spiritual decline begins when the heart is deceived. Our hearts are deceived when we entertain the lies of the enemy and truth is replaced with error. This isn't necessarily a massive error of doctrine. This is more likely a lie disguised with truth. It only ever takes a little leaven and that is all the enemy needs to deceive our hearts. Our hearts are deceived when they take hold of anything, however small, that is contrary to the Word of God.

Let us consider some examples from scripture:

1) Matthew 14:22-33
In Matthew 14 we see just how deception goes from our head to our heart. When Peter walked on the water to Jesus everything was going fine until he started to believe the thoughts the enemy put in his mind. When Peter took his eyes of the Lord and focused on the wind and waves he began to believe the lies of Satan. He allowed the thoughts of the enemy to enter his heart and he began to believe that the power of the waves was greater than the power of Jesus and he began to sink. Up until that point Peter had no problem walking on the water in the midst of the storm because his heart hadn't been deceived. Peter took his eyes off Jesus and allowed the truth of God to be corrupted by the lies of the enemy.

2) Genesis 3:1-7
In the garden of Eden Adam and Eve had their hearts deceived when they allowed the lies of the enemy to replace the Word of truth God had spoken to them. The enemy's words were meditated upon and allowed to move from the head to the heart and replace the Words that God had spoken and placed there.

Our hearts are deceived when the thoughts of the enemy are allowed to take root in our heart. In the armour of God it speaks not only of a breastplate to protect the heart but also a helmet of salvation to protect the mind. We are to take heed because the enemy comes subtly to deceive our hearts. Both our minds and our hearts need protecting. Deception seeks to lodge in our minds and move to our hearts. Once this occurs our hearts are deceived.

2. Ye turn aside
and ye turn aside,

The second step of decline is that we turn aside. When we fail to take heed and our hearts are deceived, we believe the lie and stray from the path of truth. This is the start of the turn away from the Lord. When our hearts are deceived, we stray from the narrow path that leads to life and end up on the wide path of destruction. In life there is only ever two directions. We are either walking towards God or away from Him. We can choose to turn in either direction. In repentance we turn back to God, but in spiritual decline we turn away from Him. Once our hearts have strayed our feet will naturally follow.

3. And serve other gods.
and serve other gods,

As we touched on earlier, that which we serve is that which has the priority in our lives. We cannot serve two masters. Once our hearts have been deceived and we hold the lie in greater steed than the truth, we turn from God and our service moves with us. This is not necessarily talking about idol worship, although it can be. It means that whatever holds our attention the most is the thing that we are serving the most. We may not even know we are doing it. Our service will be determined by our stance and what's in our hearts.

4. And worship
and worship them

The end result of spiritual decline. Service and worship are closely linked throughout the Word of God. Worship is always the result of that which we hold most dear in our lives. When our hearts are deceived, we turn from God, focusing in on the lie and giving it all that we have. Worship is the final step of spiritual decline when we fail to take heed.

Spiritual decline occurs when we fail to take heed when we are walking in the blessings of the Lord. Spiritual decline starts when deception enters our hearts. We then turn, serve and worship that which has replaced the truth of the Lord. The call of the Lord is for His people to take heed. He implores us as His children to take heed.

And then the LORD'S wrath be kindled against you, and he shut up the heaven, that there be no rain, and that the land yield not her fruit; and lest ye perish quickly from off the good land which the LORD giveth you. (Deu 11:17)

We see in this passage that three judgements of the Lord are mentioned. These are:

Continuation

1. Drought – Heavens shut up. No rain naturally or spiritually.
2. Famine – land yield not her fruit. Natural and spiritual man is in a hungered, weakened and oppressed state.
3. Pestilence – Perish quickly. Natural and spiritual death.

These are the exact same three judgements that we have seen continually through our study.

2 Chronicles 7	1 Kings 18	Acts 2	Deuteronomy 11
Shut up heaven that there be no rain – drought	The rains were shut up for three and a half years – Israel was in drought	Natural Drought Spiritual drought of the Spirit and the Word	Heavens Shut up
If I command locusts to devour the land – lack of provision	The land was in famine – lack of provision	Natural famine Spiritual famine of the provision of the Word as our daily bread	Land yield not her fruit
Or if I send pestilence	Loss of livestock	Natural Death Spiritual Death	Ye perish quickly

There is continuity and consistency in the judgements of the Lord throughout the Word of God. The constant message of the Lord is that if you turn from Him you will experience these things. The judgements of the Lord are ever given in response to His people failing to take heed and turning from Him. In the writer's mind, the reason for the consistency and continuity of the judgments is so that we will come to recognise what the Lord is trying to say to us. The Lord's message is constant to us and He does this so that we might recognise what is happening and be able to respond quickly. He tells us what is going to happen if we turn from Him in the hope that we will understand and recognise the situation and turn back quickly.

SUMMARY of Points A and B
To date in our study we have looked at what the people of the Lord need to do in order to return to the fulness of the blessing of the Lord. In Deuteronomy we see a people who are called to continue in the blessings of God. In Deuteronomy 11:14 and 15 we read of the continued blessings of the Lord being rain, harvest and provision for life. In Deuteronomy 11:17 we read of the judgements of the Lord as being a shut heaven, no harvest and that the people would perish.

If My People

Deuteronomy 11:14, 15	**Deuteronomy 11:17**
Blessings	Judgements
Rain in due season, first and latter	Shut up heaven that there be no rain – drought
Harvest – corn, wine and oil, grass	Famine – land yield no fruit
Life for man and beast	Perish

These blessings and judgements are consistent with what we have seen revealed in the Word so far. The qualifier here, as we have discussed, is that the people of the Lord are already walking in His blessing. They are a people who are in right relationship with Him. This would equate to the fulfillment of 2 Chronicles 7 when His people have humbled themselves, prayed, sought His face and turned from their wicked ways.

The key phrase for us is in Deuteronomy 11:16 where the people are told to "take heed". The people are told to take heed and are presented with two options from this. If they were to take heed then they would continue to walk in the blessing of the Lord. On the flip side if they failed to take heed then they would open themselves to the judgements of the Lord.

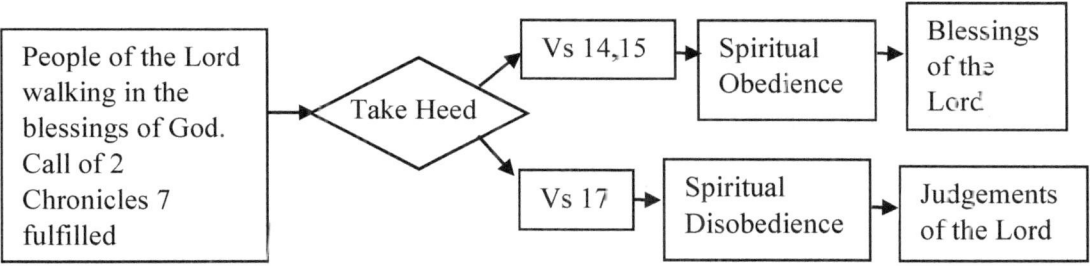

The call for the people of God is to take heed. The Lord not only reveals to us through scripture how we are to return to walking in His blessings but He also outlines for us how we are to maintain our walk in them. We are called to take head and remain in spiritual obedience unto the Lord and not fall into spiritual disobedience through spiritual decline. Through Deuteronomy so far we have seen what spiritual obedience is and we have seen what spiritual disobedience is, the question that remains is how do we fulfil the call of the Lord to take heed. This is the focus of the next part of our study as we move into verses 18-20 of Deuteronomy Chapter 11. It is here that the Lord reveals truths not only to natural Israel but also to spiritual Israel, the Church. The Lord here speaks to us about how we can make sure that we be vigilant in taking heed and not fall into the trap of complacency, which is essentially what it means to not take heed. Complacency is being so comfortable in our situation that we do not place a great value on what is before us because we fail to see the need. The Lord never wants us to be complacent. He wants us to take heed. The thief comes to steal, kill and destroy. If we are vigilant, if we stay on guard, if we remain awake and follow the truths that the Lord lays before us we ensure that we take heed. For the people of the Lord to remain in His blessings we must take heed. Let us look at how we can fulfil this.

C. <u>How We Take Heed</u>

As we have discussed already to take head is the call of the Lord to His people and His Church. The Lord's desire is for us to continue to walk in a right relationship with Him and maintain our walk in the blessings that He wants to sustain us with. Here in Deuteronomy He outlines for us just how we can take heed to ourselves. It should be noted that at the start of Deuteronomy 11 the Lord clearly outlines through Moses that He is talking to the current generation. The language of verses 1-10 constantly refers to the current generation. The message wasn't for a future generation, it was not unto their children. It was not a call that could be put off. The call was for now. The urgency was on the current generation. The call to take heed was upon them and the same call is upon us. The responsibility to take heed lies with us. It is a responsibility and a truth we must grasp hold of.

In verse 16 of Deuteronomy 11 the Lord tells us to take heed before going straight in to explain the spiritual decline that takes place if we don't take heed. There we noted that to take heed meant to hedge about, guard, to protect, to attend to. Whilst the Lord tells us to take heed here, we are not told how we are to do that. We are warned about what happens if we don't take heed but information is not given directly about how we ensure we take heed. That is until we come to verses 18 – 20 of Chapter 11.

> *Therefore shall ye lay up these my words in your heart and in your soul, and bind them for a sign upon your hand, that they may be as frontlets between your eyes. And ye shall teach them your children, speaking of them when thou sittest in thine house, and when thou walkest by the way, when thou liest down, and when thou risest up. And thou shalt write them upon the door posts of thine house, and upon thy gates: (Deu 11:18-20)*

In these verses the Lord spells out for His people just how we are to take heed. The truths He lays out here are for His people to take hold of to ensure that we continue to remain in the blessings of the Lord. If we are to take heed and not stray into complacency, then we need to take hold of what the Lord is communicating to us here. This isn't the only time the Lord spells this out for His people. In Deuteronomy 6:6-9 the Lord informs them of the exact same things.

Deuteronomy 6	**Deuteronomy 11**
(Deu 6:6) And these words, which I command thee this day, shall be in thine heart:	(Deu 11:18) Therefore shall ye lay up these my words in your heart and in your soul, …

(Deu 6:8) And thou shalt bind them for a sign upon thine hand, and they shall be as frontlets between thine eyes.	…and bind them for a sign upon your hand, that they may be as frontlets between your eyes.
(Deu 6:7) And thou shalt teach them diligently unto thy children, and shalt talk of them when thou sittest in thine house, and when thou walkest by the way, and when thou liest down, and when thou risest up.	(Deu 11:19) And ye shall teach them your children, speaking of them when thou sittest in thine house, and when thou walkest by the way, when thou liest down, and when thou risest up
(Deu 6:9) And thou shalt write them upon the posts of thy house, and on thy gates.	(Deu 11:20) And thou shalt write them upon the door posts of thine house, and upon thy gates:

He gives the same warning to His people and lays out the same ways that they are to take heed. The Lord doesn't repeat words for the sake of it. The Lord will always use more than one instance to establish truth, it is a Biblical principle and it is exactly what He does in these passages. In Deuteronomy 6 and 11 the Lord establishes a truth that He is keen for His people to grasp the message of. It is the message of taking heed.

As we consider verses 18-20 we will see that there are three main points that the Lord outlines in order for His people to take heed. As we look at these we will also see that these three points apply to three distinct spheres of our life. As we consider these, we will look at both the application to us as individuals and also the application to the Church. The focus of this study is God's call to His Church and if His Church can take heed in these areas then it can continue to walk in the blessings of His rain, harvest and life. That is the heart and prayer of the writer.

What becomes clear as we move through these verses is the focus the Lord places on His Word. As we go through each of these three points/three spheres we will see that at the heart of each is the Word of God. The Word of God, His communication to us, is vital if we are to take heed.

1. Internal or Foundational Sphere
Therefore shall ye lay up these my words in your heart and in your soul, and bind them for a sign upon your hand, that they may be as frontlets between your eyes. (Deu 11:18)

The first sphere addresses what is at the very core. It is a heart issue and it is from here that the other spheres are impacted. Whether it be an individual or the Church, this sphere deals with what is required on the inside. The Lord here speaks to the internal environment and what is required if we are to take heed. In Deuteronomy 6 these parts are separated between vs 6 and vs 8, but in chapter 11 they are all brought together in one. As we move through this verse it will be seen that this grouping was by no means coincidental.

Continuation

a)   Lay Up the Word
Therefore shall ye lay up these My Words in your heart and in your soul

The first thing that the Lord tells us to do is to lay up His Words. This point very much focuses on the heart or the core be it in application to an individual or the Church. To lay up in your heart and soul deals with what is at the very centre of who we are and what we do.

The first call here is to lay up His Words in our hearts. In vs 16 the warning is to take heed that your hearts be not deceived. Here the call is to take heed by laying up His Words in our heart and soul. Having the Word of the Lord laid up in our heart helps prevent our hearts from being deceived. Our hearts are to be anchored in His Word. At the centre of everything that we do, at our very core is to be the Word of God. His Word is:

1)   Light – Ps 119:105, Isa 8:20, Pro 6:23
2)   Truth – John 17:17
3)   Right – Ps 33:4
4)   Pure – Ps 119:140, Pro 30:5

The list goes on, but the point is that when His Word is at our very core, our heart, then we have light, truth, rightness and purity and so on. Light exposes darkness, truth exposes error, rightness exposes error and purity exposes impurity. When we have this laid up in our hearts, we protect ourselves against the deceptiveness the enemy would try and plant there.

When we looked at how our hearts are deceived, we noted that deception seeks to enter the mind and go to the heart. It is worth noting here that the call of the Lord is not to layup knowledge of His Word in our minds, but to layup His Words in our hearts. Our hearts are able to rebuke and correct our minds. They are a guard against spiritual decline. When His Word is laid up in our hearts we are able to strongly stand against the deceptions that would be thrown at us.

For the Church this shows the necessity to be firmly built and planted on the Word of the Lord. The Word has to be at the centre of who the Church is and the strength upon which we stand. From this core the rest of Church activities need to flow.

In Matthew Chapter 7 we are presented with the parable of the wise and foolish builders. Here the Lord talks about the wise builder who built his house upon the rock. When the storms came the house was able to stand because of its foundations. He then compares this to the foolish builder who built his house upon the sand. When the storms came against this house it fell because its foundations were weak. The keys for this parable are to be found in vs 24 and 26:

***Therefore whosoever heareth these sayings of mine, and doeth them**, I will liken him unto a wise man, which built his house upon a rock: (Mat 7:24)*

***And every one that heareth these sayings of mine, and doeth them not**, shall be likened unto a foolish man, which built his house upon the sand: (Mat 7:26)*

The distinction between the two builders is seen in their obedience or disobedience to the Word of God. What made the wise man's foundation strong was his obedience to the Word. He heard the Word and he acted according to the Word. In other words, he obeyed what he heard. It is this obedience that is likened to the foundation of rock. At the core of the building, what everything else was built upon was the Word.

For the Church to be able to stand and take heed it must of necessity have at its very core the Word of the Lord and obedience to it. It is this and this alone that will hold it strong in times of uncertainty and protect it from storms of deception. The Word is to be the immovable strong, sure foundation in our lives.

The Word is to be what are hearts are to be composed of. It is to be laid up and stored in our heart and soul. The Word at our very core protects us from being deceived.

b)   Bind the Word
... and bind them for a sign upon your hand... (Deu 11:18)

The Word of the Lord was to be bound to the hands of the Israelites. In our days people write notes on their hands as a prompt to remember something that they have to do. That is the essence of what is being said here. The call here to the people of God is to constantly remember the Word of God. Whenever we remember something we bring back that memory to the forefront of our minds. To have this constant reminder of the Word of God is to keep His Words at the forefront of our minds and all that we do.

The Word is not something just to be read and stored away. We need to be reminding ourselves of the truths of the Word daily. That is how we take heed, by keeping the truth of the Lord at the forefront of our minds.

For the Church it speaks of the need to constantly bring to remembrance the truths of the Word. These are the reasons we believe and do the things we do, they are based in the Word of the Lord. This stirs us to remembrance and fulfils the symbolic act of binding His Word to our hands.

By laying up His Words in our hearts we protect our hearts from deception. By keeping His Word constantly in remembrance we protect our minds. It is to be a

Continuation

repeated action. Each day we are to bring the truths of the Word to the fore front of our minds. We do this daily to constantly remind ourselves.

c)   Keep the Word before your eyes
That they may be as frontlets between your eyes… (Deuteronomy 11:18)

The call here is to keep His Word constantly before our eyes. With His Words constantly before our eyes it is continually coming through the eye gate to our minds. His Word is to be in our hearts, it is to be constantly remembered and it is to be ever before our eyes. His Words before our eyes brings freshness to our walks.

For the individual it speaks of the need to be daily reading the Word of the Lord. As we set aside that time to read His Word, we keep it before our eyes. As we keep it before our eyes it helps to prompt our memory on the truths of God. As our memory is prompted, we lay up the truths of His Word in our hearts.

For the Church it speaks of the necessity of the Word whenever we come together. This is not speaking of religious presentations of scripture verses, but life-giving messages based on the Word of the Lord.

We see here the protection from deception. His Word is before our eye gate, remembered in our minds and stored in our heart. The three areas deception tries to target are safeguarded against. The Word of the Lord has to be foundational in our lives and Churches, it has to be constantly brought to remembrance and it must always be brought to the attention of our eyes. By keeping the Word before our eyes, and constantly remembering it in our minds we protect our hearts by ensuring it stays laid up there. The Word of the Lord is key for the Church and us as individuals to take heed on an internal level. The Word has to be the essence of all that we are.

The Word of the Lord is to be ever before our eyes, at the forefront of our minds and written upon our hearts (Pro 7:2-3. Heb 8:10, 10;16). The fact is that truth and deception both enter the heart the same way. As we saw with Jacob deception targets a "gate" to get into the mind and infiltrate the heart. The defence against this is by making sure these three areas are ever guarded by truth.

Area	Deception	Truth
Gate (Ear, Eye, Nose, Touch, Smell)	Seeks to enter via one of these gates	Need to keep on guard with truth at these gates
Mind	Seeks to push truth to the back of the mind	Need to keep truth at the forefront of our mind

| Heart | Seeks to push truth out of the heart and replace it with error | Need to have truth written on and laid in our hearts and souls |

The safeguard against deception is always uncompromising truth. His Word is truth and it is this we are to safeguard ourselves with. It is by holding tightly on to truth that we take heed.

In this internal or foundational sphere we have seen that the Word of God is to be our utmost priority. Jesus said that out of the abundance of the heart the mouth speaks (Luke 6:45). This is a truth so clearly evidenced in the lives and hearts of all people. That which has prominence in our hearts dictates how we live our lives. The writer would also put forth that out of the foundation (heart) of the Church, the Church acts. If the Word is not out our foundation and protected there, being constantly remembered and put before our eyes, then how the Church acts and operates will be affected. The Word must of necessity be at the core of all that we are. We are called to take heed and it starts in this internal sphere, the foundational core. Take heed to the Word.

2. Middle or Influential Sphere
And ye shall teach them your children, speaking of them when thou sittest in thine house, and when thou walkest by the way, when thou liest down, and when thou risest up. (Deu 11:19)

The responsibility to take heed continues. We have looked at the responsibility we have to ourselves, now we look at the responsibility we have to others. This in an outworking of the inner sphere, the internal or foundational sphere. In that sphere we saw that the core was the Word. In this sphere is the beginning of the outworking of the Word. We are not called to simply hold the Word, we are called to disperse it and our first responsibility is to touch those closest to us. As we consider verse 18 there are a number of points for us to digest.

a) Teach them to your Children
And ye shall teach them your children,

The first action of outworking that we see is the need to teach them to your children. In verse 18 the Lord has spoken about the importance of His Words being in our hearts, at the forefront of our minds and ever before our eyes. That addresses the internal state of things. Here though the Lord addresses how we communicate the Word to those who are in our circle of influence. The call for us to take heed is not one reserved for our generation. It is a call to take heed for the future generations as well. The responsibility of us as believers and upon the Church is to go from strength to strength and we do this by understanding the need to take heed for those who come after us. This process starts when the truths at our foundation are communicated to those closest to us. Let us consider what this process involves:

1) Teach them.
And ye shall teach

Teaching starts with a subject matter. We cannot teach anyone if we do not know what we are supposed to be teaching them. The call here is to teach the Word of the Lord. So how do we teach the Words of the Lord.

In order to teach someone fully there is a gap that has to be bridged between the communicator and the person receiving the communication. This gap is known as the communication gap. A communication gap is anything that separates the teacher from the student be it language, experience, age, understanding etc. For anything to be taught the message has to be communicated in such a way that the communication gap is bridged and the person not only receives what was communicated, but they are able to rehearse what was taught. The rehearsing is the most important part. For someone to have truly been taught, they are able to recount what has been taught to them. This is why schools, colleges, universities etc all have exams, it is to make sure that students have actually learned what they have been taught and are able to demonstrate that.

It should also be noted that teaching is far more than words. Speaking is definitely a part of teaching, but it is not the only part. Teaching involves meeting the individual at their level, speaking, demonstrating, listening, correcting, questions, follow-up, repeating, nurturing development and walking with.

A year one teacher doesn't come to their class with a high school syllabus. They meet the students at their level, communicate truths to them, demonstrate the truths practically, listen to the student's responses and provide correction when needed. They will ask questions to try and help stimulate thinking, follow up with students in the following days and weeks to make sure they have remembered. They will repeat where necessary, nurture their development and walk with them through to the next stage of their journey.

Jesus is the best example of this we could ever look to. Jesus in calling the twelve disciples took unschooled, uneducated individuals and over three and a half years of teaching them, discipled them into mighty men of God. As we read through the gospels, we read how Jesus taught them simply, using parables and then explaining them. He answered their questions, came alongside them, corrected them when necessary, asked them questions to cause them to think and above all practiced and demonstrated that which He preached. Jesus met the disciples at their level but brought them to a higher one. He exemplifies what it means to teach.

For Christians and the Church, we have an obligation to teach. The Bible refers to this as discipleship. When we disciple, we literally come along someone at whatever stage of life they are at and meet them there with the Word of God. We speak the truth to them, we demonstrate it through our lives, we listen to their responses correcting where needed and asking questions to prompt their thinking. We follow-up with and walk beside them as they develop in their spiritual journey. This is the essence of teaching.

Teaching is a way of life. The subject matter is always the Word of the Lord. Our lives are to be a living lesson for those closest to us, but the Word needs to flow through our actions just as much as it does from our mouths. Some of the greatest lessons will come when we never actually speak. People will observe us and learn. The Word of God is to outpour from us into every aspect of our lives and actions.

2) Children
And ye shall teach them to your children

The responsibility is to teach, the subject matter is the Word of God and the audience is our children. Children speak of the next generation, that which comes after us. In the writer's opinion this has an application both in the natural and the spiritual.

i) Natural
We have an obligation to our natural children to instruct them and raise them in the ways of the Lord.

> *Train up a child in the way he should go: and when he is old, he will not depart from it. (Pro 22:6)*

This is a responsibility that rests upon every Christian parent. As parents we have the opportunity to have the greatest impact on our children. We spend the most time with them and they observe our lives, how we act, react and what we are like behind closed doors when no one else can see. As parents our role is not just to tell them about the Word of the Lord but to demonstrate it to them. We have the responsibility to disciple our children in the ways of the Lord and our great hope is that they will continue with Him in their adult lives.

ii) Spiritual

Continuation

Just as there are children in the natural so too are there children in the spiritual. New and young believers need to be taught and raised in the ways of the Lord by those who are more matured in the faith. The difference here is that the "child" status refers to their period of time as a believer and not their actual age. A sixty year old who comes to Christ still needs to be taught as a spiritual child the same as a twenty year old who comes to Christ. They need to be taught the Word of the Lord and discipled in their Christian walk.

This is a responsibility that rests upon the Church. As new Christians are born into the Kingdom of God they need to be nurtured and taught the Word of God. Just as natural children are raised so too are spiritual. The same foundation that is in our heart needs to be in theirs. Spiritual children will start on milk before moving to the meat of the Word. As they are nurtured and discipled they grow into spiritual adults who themselves will disciple future generations.

b) Speaking
speaking of them when thou sittest in thine house

The Word of the Lord is to be spoken in our houses. We are to speak it in the houses in which we live and also in the House of the Lord, the Church. The Word needs to be spoken, it is to be the language of our lips.

Whilst teaching involves speaking we are not always teaching when we speak. The Word of the Lord should be our native language. The Word tells us that out of the abundance of the heart the mouth speaks. If His Word is at the core of our hearts then His Word should naturally flow out. Our conversation should be tinged with the perfume of His Word.
The Word also says that there is life and death in the power of the tongue (Proverbs 18:21). Our Words are to be life to the next generation. As they sit in our natural and spiritual houses there must of necessity be an impartation of life that can only come through the Word of the Lord. As we speak the truth of the Word of the Lord there is an impartation of life to those who hear it.

For the Church the language of the House has to be the Word of God. It must be our native language. It is the language we are to communicate with and speak to our children so they so will be able to learn it. Just as natural children learn to speak by hearing the language and words that are spoken around them, so to do spiritual. Our spiritual children need to hear the Word of God in order for them to be able to speak it themselves.

c) Walk
And (speaking) when thou walkest by the way

The call here is to speak about them with our children when we are walking by the way. In the writer's mind this is not just talking about having a conversation as we stroll along, it is referring to the way in which we conduct our lives. Throughout the Word of God the way one walks speaks of how they lived. The call here is for us when we teach the next generation to not just use words but also actions. Words are empty if we do not exemplify them. We can speak as much as we want but if our lives do not reflect what we are broadcasting then all we will impart is hypocrisy. Our lives are to be a living portrayal of the truth we believe and speak about. We are to teach the Word, we are to speak the Word and we are to demonstrate the Word. We are to be living examples of that which is in our hearts and that which we teach and speak. The way we live our lives is to validate that which comes out of our mouths.

In 2 Peter 2:5 Noah is referred to as a preacher of righteousness. The word for preacher as used here means a herald of divine truth and is only ever interpreted with the English word preacher. Noah was a great man of God and, as we noted before, is only one of two men recorded as having walked with God. As the writer has looked at Noah, he has not found a single sermon of Noah's recorded in the Bible. Noah spent one hundred years in building the ark and no doubt he would have addressed those around him at some stage, but this is not the sole thing that made Noah a preacher of righteousness. Noah's preaching was shown forth by the way he lived and the way he walked. Noah's preaching was demonstrated through his works, his work and his actions of faith. The way in which Noah conducted his life was a message to all of those around Him. Noah communicated or taught the truths of the Lord through his life and the way he lived.

In the parable of the good Samaritan, we read of a man who was robbed and left lying in a ditch. Throughout the course of the day three individuals walked along the way where he was. There was a Priest, a Levite and a Samaritan. Now the Priest and Levite would have been well versed in the law and no doubt had taught others about its importance. Their lives though didn't reflect the truths that they spoke of. Of these three only one stopped and sought to the needs of the individual. The walk of the good Samaritan demonstrated the truths of what it meant to love one's neighbour.

It is not just about what we know and what we can impart, it is also about what we demonstrate. What others can see from the way we walk. As we noted earlier, to walk in His ways is to walk as He walks. It is to follow in His footsteps. Our lives are a living testimony of what we believe. The fruit of our lives is to be a testimony of His Word.

d)   Liest and Risest
(Speaking of them) when thou liest down, and when thou risest up

Continuation

When thou liest and risest is an interesting term. It refers to the end of the day or the evening and the start of the day or the morning. It is interesting to note that this is the same order that is given in Genesis during the creation of the world. There the wording is continually:

*And God called the light Day, and the darkness he called Night. And **the evening and the morning were the first day**. (Gen 1:5)*
See also (Gen 1:8,13,19,23,31)

The evening and morning mark the end of one day and the beginning of another.

This verse of Deuteronomy we are looking at was written in the time of the Tabernacle of Moses where God had explained to the Israelites how they were to live, worship and obey Him. Throughout the scriptures that cover this period we see this theme of the morning and evening occur frequently. We see from the Word that the Lord introduced to the nation of Israel ordinances of worship linked to these times of the morning and evening. The Israelites lives were marked with things that happened as they rose and as they lay down in relation to the Lord. There is a mindset here that the Israelites would have understood.

In the Tabernacle of Moses there were a number of things that were done both in the morning and the evening:

1) There were the morning and evening sacrifices known as the daily burnt offerings
Numbers 28:1-8

On a daily basis the Priests would offer upon the brazen altar a lamb with its accompaniments in the morning and in the evening. The sacrifices were identical, and they were done in the evening and the morning according to the Word of the Lord. Israel would start their day with worship of the Lord and close their day with worship of the Lord. Part of the reason for this continual worship was to ensure that the fire on the brazen altar that was divinely lit on the day of dedication never went out.

2) The lampstand was attended to morning and evening.
Ex 30:7-8, Lev 24:3

Every morning and every evening the priests would attend to the lamps of the lampstand. They would trim the wicks and supply oil. This was again done to ensure that the light never went out. The Priests would attend to this daily.

All of these things were part of the daily priestly ministrations. They formed part of the Israelites worship of the Lord. Whilst they were initiated in the Tabernacle of Moses they are truths that flow through scripture. It is this truth that the writer believes is being communicated here. The Worship of the Lord is to be exhibited in our lives when we lie and when we rise. He is literally meant to be the bookends of our day. We wake up and seek Him afresh, we lay down thanking Him for the day. By doing this, we not only ensure that we continually fuel the fire in our lives but we demonstrate to our children the imperative need of having the Lord as the brackets to our day. Our relationship with Him is not something we try and squeeze into our lives. He is the priority. He is our first thought and our last thought. We seek Him in the morning and we seek Him at night. The psalmist puts it like this:

> **Evening**, and **morning**, and at **noon**, will I pray, and cry aloud: and he shall hear my voice. (Psa 55:17)

The Lord in Proverbs adds this thought:

> *I love them that love me; and those that seek me **early** shall find me. (Pro 8:17)*

The next generation is to look upon our lives and observe how we conduct our relationship with the Lord. We should be demonstrating what we are teaching them to do.

The responsibility is upon us to teach the Word of the Lord to the next generation, both our children in the natural and our children in the spiritual. We are to teach them, communicating truth to them and bridging any gap in understanding. They are to hear the Word of the Lord as the language of our lips as we speak throughout the day in every situation. We are to demonstrate the truth of the Word through the way we act. Our lives are to set forth the example of seeking the Lord in the evening and morning as we show Him to be our priority.

Part of the call to take heed involves teaching the next generation in the ways they should go. This not only safeguards them to be able to hopefully remain in the blessings of the Lord, but it also safeguards us. As we constantly teach our children the truths of the Lord, they stay ever fresh and in the forefront of our minds. The act of teaching is a constant reminder of what we believe and why we believe it. In this way teaching not only helps us to take heed it is also a safeguard for the next generation. When we teach the next generation, we impart to them the need to take heed and we see the generations go from strength to strength. When we fail to teach the next generation, the truths are lost, the generations wander and they fall into the judgements of the Lord.

The vital necessity of teaching the next generation and imparting to them the lessons to take heed so they may in turn teach it to their children is no better illustrated than in

Continuation

Judges Chapter 2. There we read of the death of Joshua and those of his generation. This was the generation that had inherited the promised land. Joshua and Caleb had been part of the deliverance of Israel from Egypt. The generation they led into the promised land had not witnessed the miracles of Egypt but they had seen the hand of the Lord move in power as they crossed the Jordan and took hold of the inheritance that the Lord had for them. Sadly though, once this generation passed away we read an incredibly sad passage of scripture:

> *And Joshua the son of Nun, the servant of the LORD, died, being an hundred and ten years old. And they buried him in the border of his inheritance in Timnathheres, in the mount of Ephraim, on the north side of the hill Gaash. And also all that generation were gathered unto their fathers:* **_and there arose another generation after them, which knew not the LORD, nor yet the works which he had done for Israel_**. *And the children of Israel did evil in the sight of the LORD, and served Baalim: And they forsook the LORD God of their fathers, which brought them out of the land of Egypt, and followed other gods, of the gods of the people that were round about them, and bowed themselves unto them, and provoked the LORD to anger. (Jdg 2:8-12)*

How could this happen? This happened so shortly into Israel's time in the promised land. How could a generation arise who knew not the Lord? The Israelites where comfortable in the land of promise. The victories had been won, the battles were over. They had become complacent and with that they failed to take heed. They failed to teach the Word of the Lord to their children. A generation can only arise not knowing the Lord or His works if they have not been taught about them. Paul in Romans sums it up like this:

> *For whosoever shall call upon the name of the Lord shall be saved. How then shall they call on him in whom they have not believed? And how shall they believe in him of whom* ***they have not heard****? And how shall they hear without a* ***preacher****? And how shall they preach, except they be sent? As it is written, How beautiful are the feet of them that preach the gospel of peace, and bring glad tidings of good things! (Rom 10:13-15)*

To each of us who believe, to the Church at large the call is to preach and teach the Word of the Lord to our children. We have been sent by the Lord with this mandate. We have the call and responsibility to teach the Word of the Lord to our natural and spiritual children. It is the mandate to take heed and one that rests upon each and every one of us.

3. Outer / Evangelical Sphere
And thou shalt write them upon the door posts of thine house, and upon thy gates: (Deu 11:20)

Having looked at the internal and middle spheres we now move to the outer sphere which the writer has also dubbed the evangelical sphere. The thoughts behind this will hopefully become clear as we move through this verse.

The question for us to consider here is what does it mean to write them on the door posts of our house and upon thy gates? What is the truth of the Lord here? In considering this the writer was led to some scriptures in the Word that the Lord quickened to him. These provided some insights into what the writer believes the Lord is saying here.

    a)   Doors

Exodus 12:7,13

During the original Passover with Israel in Egypt, the Israelites were to take the blood of the Passover lamb and sprinkle it upon the lintels of the door to their houses with hyssop. They applied the blood to the two side posts and the top of the door in a triune application. The Israelites then dwelt within the protection of that blood-stained door as the judgement of the Lord came upon the nation of Egypt. The angel flew through the land of Egypt and as he looked upon the houses, the blood stood as a sign to him. From the outside the angel saw the blood upon the door and passed over the house. The blood upon the door was not only a declaration that the family had partaken of the Passover lamb it was also a sign to anyone outside who saw it. It was both a sign and a declaration.

    b)   Gates

In Joshua 6 we read that as Joshua and the Israelites came to the city of Jericho they found it tightly shut up. Jericho was a walled city that had gates. These gates allowed entry and exit to the city. In this case the closed gates allowed no one to enter.

In Judges 16 we read that Samson tore down the gates of Gaza in order to escape the city and the men that were lying in wait for him there. Here the gates prevented exit.

Door posts and gates mark points of entry into a city or a house. They allow entry and exit and also prohibit the same. They are the way in and they are the way out. There is a two directional focus here. Coming in and going out.

To write upon the doors and gates is to communicate a message for anyone coming in and going out. It is a sign, a message, a truth for those on the outside and those on the inside.

To write the Words of the Lord on our doorposts and gates speaks of two things:

    a)   Entry

It is a declaration. To write the words on the door and gates is to declare what is held to and believed by those who indwell there. It is a sign to all who are on the outside that as for me and my house we will serve the Lord (Josh 24:15). Anyone who comes into that house or city knows the truths by which it lives. Anyone who entered the blood stained door during the Passover knew what was believed by those on the inside. It spoke truth to all those who saw it. This is what we believe.

A city on a hill is not meant be hidden and nor is the light within us meant to be put under a bushel (Matthew 5:14 -15). Within our communities and in the lives of the unsaved people we encounter we are to stand unashamedly as representations of the truths we believe. Anyone that comes into our paths, homes or Churches knows what they are coming into. In declaring we stand, and all those who come and enter our doors understand what they are coming into.

b)   Exit

It speaks of communicating the Word of the Lord to those who are outside. It speaks of spreading the message that is in our internal sphere out into the external. As we go out, we take the truths written on the doors with us.

The internal sphere represents us and our hearts. The middle sphere is those closest to us, our natural and spiritual children. This outer sphere is those people who are unsaved and whom we have contact with. As we go out into this sphere we take the truths of the Word with us, evangelising to those we encounter.

Part of taking heed is to never be satisfied with the way things are when there are those around us who do not know the Lord. As we go out of "our doors" and "our gates" we go as ambassadors of the truths our houses and Churches stand for. As we go out we go under the banner of the Lord as His representatives to a world that needs Him.

In times of blessing an outward focus prevents us from becoming self-satisfied, as we observe and understand the greatness of the need around us. Part of taking heed is continuing to communicate the truths of God's Word to those who need it whilst at the same time unashamedly standing for what we believe. As people come into the sphere they see it, as we go out into that sphere we declare it.

From our consideration of how we take heed we have seen that here is an inner, a middle and an outer sphere, as highlighted by the following diagram:

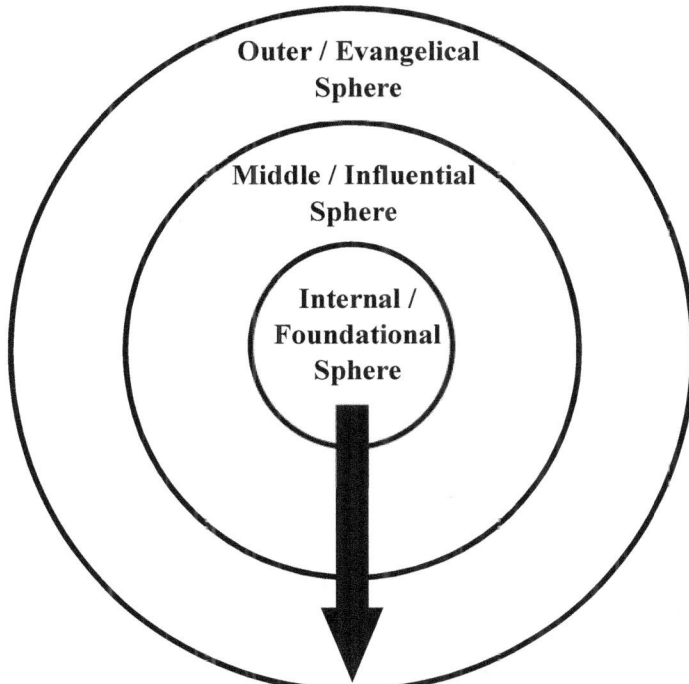

From the Inside Out

The call to take heed starts with ourselves and the need to safeguard the truths in our hearts. From there we step out into the middle sphere where we take heed by teaching the truths of the Word to our children, natural and spiritual. Finally, we step out into the outer sphere or the evangelical sphere. It is here that we take the message of the good news of the gospel out to those who need it.

The call is to take heed, but there is a threefold application with this. What we must always keep in mind is that this call works from the inside out. We need to make sure we are taking heed at the internal level if we are to have any impact on the other two spheres. We are vessels created to outpour, but we can only continue to outpour as we continue to receive from Him who is the source. As we press into the Lord, we make sure the flow continues outward.

Whilst we have highlighted the importance of the internal sphere above, we must always remember that the call is threefold. By constantly keeping this in mind we ensure that we remain balanced. The reality is that for the people of God to take heed as He has called us, we must constantly keep all of these three spheres in focus. We cannot afford to neglect any of these spheres, for to do so is to not take heed.

Continuation

D. <u>The Result</u>
That your days may be multiplied, and the days of your children, in the land which the LORD sware unto your fathers to give them, as the days of heaven upon the earth. (Deu 11:21)

If we can grasp the message to take heed then the promise of blessing is ours. It is not a blessing just for ourselves, but also for our children. As we take heed and apply these truths to the three spheres of our lives that we have discovered we ensure that not only we, but our children and hopefully our children's children remain in the promised blessing of the Lord.

The crux of this is summed up in Deuteronomy 11:26-28:

> *Behold, I set before you this day a blessing and a curse; A blessing, if ye obey the commandments of the LORD your God, which I command you this day: And a curse, if ye will not obey the commandments of the LORD your God, but turn aside out of the way which I command you this day, to go after other gods, which ye have not known. (Deu 11:26-28)*

May our testimony ever be that having returned to the Lord we ever apply the lessons of taking heed and always remain in the blessings of the Lord. What marvellous things the Lord has for His Church when His people remain in His blessings. When His people take heed they continue to remain in His blessings. If we as the people of God, His Church, can apply this message to take heed then our days of blessing will be multiplied.

If My People

CONTINUATION SUMMARY

In this section we focused on the "what happens next". Having at the beginning of this study looked at and discovered how the people of the Lord return to the blessings of the Lord, in this section we focused on how the people of the Lord remain in His blessings. To have the people of the Lord return to the fulness of His blessings and to see them continue in them from generation to generation is the heart and prayer of the writer.

It was with this in mind that we looked at Deuteronomy 11 and also considered Deuteronomy 6. There we discovered the truths the Lord had outlined for His people to continue on the path of blessing. As we considered these passages, we broke our study into three sections.

A. <u>The Promise of Continued Blessing</u>

Between Deuteronomy 10 and Deuteronomy 11 the Lord outlines five requirements upon His people. They are to:
1. Fear Him – a reverential fear of the Lord based on who He is.
2. Walk in His Ways – our walk is to reflect His.
3. Love Him – Heart issue.
4. Serve Him – He is to be our number one priority.
5. Obey Him – His commandments of loving God and loving man.

These requirements are the way in which the people of the Lord are to live. It is to this standard that His people are called to return in 1 Chronicles. If His people remain in these requirements, then the promise of the Lord is the blessings of:
1. Rain
2. Harvest
3. Life

These blessings are not only a response to His people responding to the judgements of the Lord and seeking Him afresh but continue as His people diligently hearken unto the Lord and His commandments in love. The Lord has blessing for His people and these three blessings that He has outlined have both a natural and spiritual application to the Church.

B. <u>The warning of judgement</u>

Whilst outlining the promises for continued obedience the Lord warns of the possibility of His judgements if His people fail to take heed and fall into spiritual decline. This process of spiritual decline occurs through:

1. Hearts deceived

Deception gets into our hearts through deceiving our senses and entering our minds. From the mind it travels to the heart and pushes out truth.

Continuation Summary

2. Ye turn aside

In repentance we turn back to God but in spiritual decline we turn away from Him. Once our hearts have strayed our feet will naturally follow.

3. And serve other gods.

Whatever holds our attention the most is the thing that we are serve the most. We may not even know we are doing it.

4. And worship

The end result of spiritual decline.

Spiritual decline occurs when we fail to take heed when we are walking in the blessings of the Lord. Once spiritual decline reaches its climax, we find ourselves in the judgements of the Lord. We see that these are the same judgements already considered in our study to date. The fact they are again mentioned here further confirms the truths we have discussed. These judgements of the Lod are:

1. Drought – Heavens shut up
2. Famine – Land yield not her fruit
3. Pestilence – Perish quickly

Again, these judgements have both a natural and a spiritual application to the people of God and the Church.

The message from points A and B is that when the people of the Lord are walking in the blessings of the Lord they need to take heed lest they fall. The question remains, how do we take heed?

C. How We Take Heed

We take heed by giving attention to the three spheres that the Lord outlines for us in Deuteronomy 11:18-20. At the heart of each of these sphere's is the Word of God.

1. Internal or Foundational Sphere

The first sphere addresses what is at the very core. It is a heart issue and it is from here that the other spheres are impacted.

   a) Lay Up the Word

   The Word is to be what comprises our heart, it is to be laid up and stored in our heart and soul. The Word at our very core protects us from being deceived.

   b) Bind the Word

   To bind the Word is to constantly remind ourselves of the Word of the Lord and keep it at the forefront of our minds. It is to constantly bring to remembrance the truths of the Word.

c)   Keep the Word before your eyes

His Word is to be in our hearts, it is to be constantly remembered and it is to be ever before our eyes. His Word before our eyes brings freshness to our walks on a daily basis.

2.   Middle or Influential Sphere

This in an outworking of the inner sphere, the internal or foundational sphere. We are not called to simply hold the Word, we are called to disperse it and our first responsibility is to touch those closest to us.

a)   Teach them to your Children

The call of the Lord is to teach His Words to our children. There is a responsibility on the current generation to impart to the next.

1) Teach them.

Teaching involves meeting the individual at their level, speaking, demonstrating, listening, correcting, questioning, following-up, repeating, nurturing developing and walking with.

2) Children

i) Natural

We have an obligation to our natural children to instruct them and raise them in the ways of the Lord.

ii) Spiritual

New and young believers need to be taught and raised in the ways of the Lord by those who are more matured in the faith.

b)   Speaking

The Word of the Lord is to be spoken in our houses. We are to speak it in the houses in which we live and also in the House of the Lord, the Church. The Word needs to be spoken; it is to be the language of our lips.

c)   Walk

Our lives are to be a living portrayal of the truth we believe and speak about. We are to teach the Word, we are to speak the Word and we are to demonstrate the Word in our walks.

d)   Liest and Risest

This touches on the Old Testament priestly ministrations and applies to our times of worship in prayer and sacrifice unto the Lord. The next generation is to look upon our lives and observe how we conduct our relationship with the Lord. Our days are to be bookended by the Lord.

3.   Outer or Evangelical Sphere

Continuation Summary

The outer sphere which the writer has also dubbed the evangelical sphere. The doors and gates referred to in this section have a twofold application of people coming in and believers going out.

a)   Entry

It is a declaration. To write the Words on the door and gates is to declare what is held to and believed by those within this sphere. Those that come in know what they are entering in to.

b)   Exit

It speaks of communicating the Word of the Lord to those who are outside. We take the Word with us as we go out into the world, proclaiming His word to those who need to hear it.

D. The Result

If we can grasp the message to take heed, then the promise of blessing is ours. It is not a blessing just for ourselves, but also for our children. If we take heed, then we remain in the blessings of the Lord.

CONCLUSION

The promised blessings of rain, harvest and life are not just an initial reward from the Lord for a people that return to seeking Him with all their heart, soul and strength. They are a continual blessing from the Lord if His people and Church listen to the message of the Lord and take heed. When we return and take heed to continue in the ways of the Lord, the rains of the Lord keep coming. That is the writer's heart for the Church and indeed the purpose of this study. Manifestations of revival are amazing and the writer's heart is to see that come to the Church. But the call of the Lord for His Church is to walk in the fulness of His blessings not just for a day, week, month or year, but to permanently dwell in the promised land that He has for us from the current generation until His return.

As we have considered Deuteronomy 11 we discovered that the Lord outlines the exact same judgements as we saw in Chronicles. The Lord though not only tells us that they come but also tells us why they come. The judgements of the Lord are ever a reaction to the action of His people. Isaiah tells us:

> *With my soul have I desired thee in the night; yea, with my spirit within me will I seek thee early:* ***for when thy judgments are in the earth, the inhabitants of the world will learn righteousness. (Isa 26:9)***

As we have seen throughout our study of both the passages in Chronicles and Deuteronomy, the judgements of the Lord come when His people forsake Him and are brought to try and get their attention. The judgements of the Lord are ever a call to His people. His desire is for us to walk in His blessings and His judgements come to try and get us back to that point. The Lord's hope for us is not just that His people would return to Him afresh but that we would take heed to remain in His blessings forever.

It is the writer's firm belief, as stated already, that the Lord is wanting His Church to seek Him afresh and enter into the fulness of His blessings. He would have us not enter this promised land momentarily, but dwell there permanently and as we do this, take heed and see His light expand throughout the nations, from the inner spheres to the outer spheres. The Lord has much for His Church, and if we can grasp hold of the message to take heed, applying it to the three spheres we have discussed, the world around us will be greatly impacted.

SUPPLEMENTAL A

Balance of the Spirit and the Word

In the last section we looked at the need for believers and the Church to take heed. As we did this we discovered the overwhelming importance of the Word of God. The Word has to be at the core of who we are, we have to raise our children in it and it is with the Word that we are to outreach to those around us. The emphasis is very much on the Word.

The writer of this study is one who loves the Word of God, who loves to read it and loves to study it. In saying that though it is the writer's belief that the Word goes hand and hand with the Spirit. In regard to the balance of the Spirit and the Word the writer was once told:

Too much Word and people will dry up
Too much Spirit and people will blow up
Combine the two and people will grow up.

So whilst we focused solely on the Word in the previous section it is the writer's firm belief that this focus on the Word goes hand and hand with a focus on the Spirit. The two go together. This is not just the writer's view, but is a truth demonstrated throughout scripture. It is not the writer's intention to do a complete study on this subject but it would be beneficial to consider a few scriptures which highlight this point:

A. <u>The Word and Spirit at Creation</u>
In the beginning God created the heaven and the earth. And the earth was without form, and void; and darkness was upon the face of the deep. And the Spirit of God moved upon the face of the waters. And God said, Let there be light: and there was light. (Gen 1:1-3)

At the very beginning we see in Genesis that there was:
1. God – In the beginning God
2. The Spirit – The Spirit of God moved upon the Waters
3. The Word – And God said, "Let there be Light" Literally the Word of God came forth. Jesus, as the Word at creation, is a thought that is confirmed by John at the start of his gospel:

In the beginning was the Word, and the Word was with God, and the Word was God. The same was in the beginning with God. All things were made by him; and without him was not any thing made that was made. (Joh 1:1-3)

Supplemental A

Jesus (The Word) and the Holy Ghost (the Spirit) are evidenced working together right at the beginning of creation. The Spirit moved upon the water, the Word come forth and creation began according to the will of God. The Word and the Spirit worked together. Both were needed and both were involved. There was balance between the two at the beginning.

B. <u>The Word and Spirit in Jesus</u>
And the Word was made flesh, and dwelt among us, (and we beheld his glory, the glory as of the only begotten of the Father,) full of grace and truth. (Joh 1:14)

For he whom God hath sent speaketh the words of God: for God giveth not the Spirit by measure unto him. (Joh 3:34)

Jesus was the Word made flesh. He was the Word incarnate. He also had the Spirit without measure. He was the fulness of the Word and at the same time He was given the Spirit without measure. He was full of the Word and full of the Spirit. The two were equally balanced within Him. He did not have one without the other. One did not have dominance over the other. The two were balanced within Him, there was fulness of both. The two worked together throughout His ministry. The words that He spoke were the Words of God and He did this through the anointing of the Spirit. The Spirit and the Word worked together.

C. <u>The Word and Spirit for believers</u>
And take the helmet of salvation, and the sword of the Spirit, which is the word of God: (Eph 6:17)

In writing to the Ephesians Paul details to them the necessity of putting on the spiritual armour of God. In his discourse he tells them to make sure they have the sword of the Spirit which is the Word of God. His words are you need the sword of the Spirit and that same sword is the Word of the God. It is one and the same thing. It is unity yet differentiation. Above all it is balance. The sword is a weapon used not only to defend, but to take ground. Believers can only take ground when they have the Word and the Spirit. The two work together as one. They are divisible yet united. To have the sword you need both the Spirit and the Word.

<u>CONCLUSION</u>
Throughout our previous section where we looked at the necessity of the Word in the three spheres detailed for us in Deuteronomy 11:18-20, whilst we never mentioned the influence of the Spirit, the writer's standpoint would be that wherever we made mention of the Word there is an equal balance and application of the Spirit. The two are inseparable for believers to be able to function in the fulness of what the Lord has called us to. The two go together and the two are balanced. The few scriptures we have looked at

further highlight this point and the reader is encouraged to go over these and see the truths that the Lord is speaking to us.

The Word and the Spirit work together. The two must always be in balance and one should never be emphasised to the detriment of the other, for this causes imbalance. There must always be a balance of Word and Spirit. The Word teaches about the Spirit and the Spirit teaches about the Word

Other Scriptures for the reader to consider: 2 Pet 1:21, Isa 59:21, Proverbs 1:23

If My People

SUPPLEMENTAL B

Spiritual Incline and Spiritual Decline

In this study we have looked at both the people of God returning to the Lord and also their need to take heed and stay there. As we have looked at 2 Chronicles 7:14 and Deuteronomy 11:16 we see an interesting contrast between spiritual incline and spiritual decline.

A. Spiritual Incline

In 2 Chronicles 7:14 we see the steps outlined for the people of the Lord to return to the blessings of the Lord. His people go from judgement to blessing if they choose these steps. It is a path that leads back to the Lord and as such the writer has called it the path of spiritual incline. These steps as outlined in 2 Chronicles 7:14 for His people are:

1. Humble yourselves
2. Pray
3. Seek My face
4. Turn from your wicked ways

These four steps, as determined by the Lord and as noted in our study, are progressive in nature. i.e. one leads to two, two leads to three etc. With each step that believers take they step back towards a closer relationship with the Lord. They also take a step back to returning to the blessing of the Lord. These steps can be seen as:

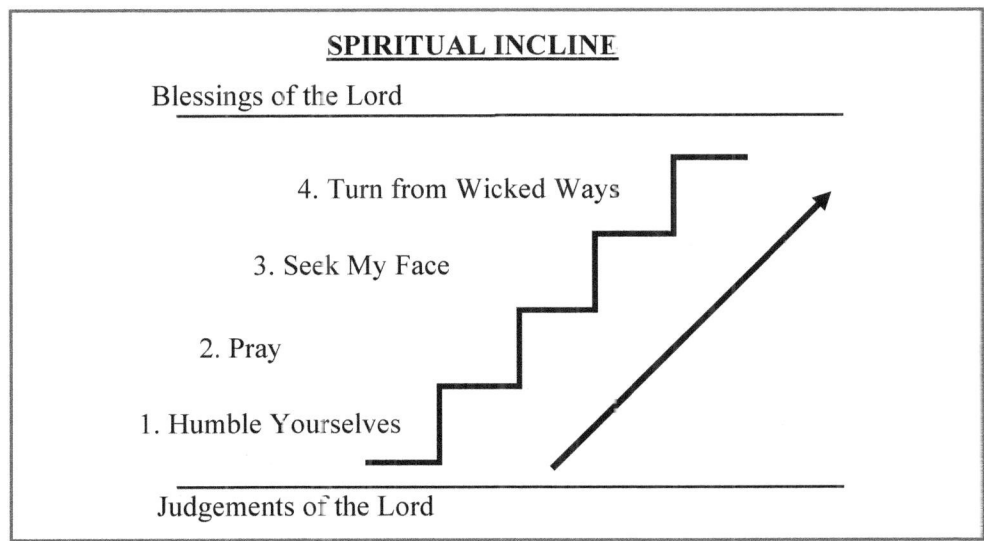

Supplemental B

B. <u>Spiritual Decline</u>
On the converse to this we see in Deuteronomy 11 the path of spiritual decline. Here the Lord outlines the steps that believers take when they step away from a right relationship with Him and step towards the judgements of the Lord. Again we see that there are four steps that His people take. These are:

1. Hearts deceived
2. Turn from
3. Serve
4. Worship

Just as with the steps of spiritual incline the steps of spiritual decline are progressive in nature. What starts in the heart can cause separation between God and man if man continues on the steps downwards.

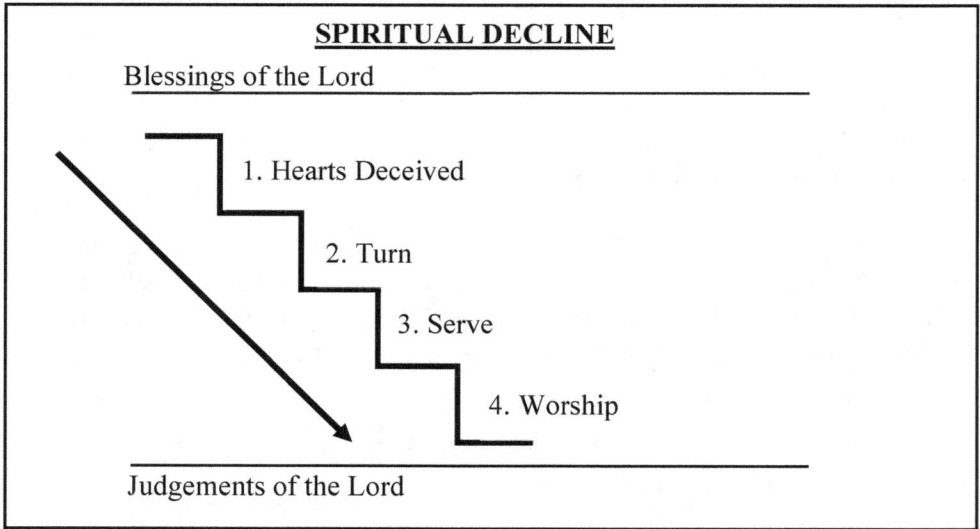

The path of spiritual decline consists of four steps that will take believers from the blessings of the Lord to His judgements. The path leads away from the Lord and His blessings.

<u>CONCLUSION</u>
The purpose of this short section is to show that the blessings or judgements of the Lord are the choice of man. God provides the opportunity for both, but it is man who chooses in which way he walks. God informs us of the steps needed to return to blessing and He also warns us to take heed of the steps that lead to spiritual decline. It is up to us as believers though to have ears to hear what the Lord is saying.

FINAL REMARKS

With my soul have I desired thee in the night; yea, with my spirit within me will I seek thee early: for when thy judgments are in the earth, the inhabitants of the world will learn righteousness. (Isa 26:9)

The purpose of this study has been to highlight what the writer believes is a call to the Church today. As we have studied His Word we have seen the necessity of His people to return to the Lord, to see His blessings, natural and spiritual, poured out upon our lands. Having done this we have then discovered what is required to remain in the promised land of blessing and ensure this continues for the generations to come.

The Lord's desire is for us to remain in His blessing. His judgements come when we fail to take heed and they come with the purpose, as Isaiah says, to draw us back to the path of righteousness and towards spiritual incline.

It is the writer's prayer that the reader has been blessed by something, however small, as they have read this book. May our paths be ever on the incline and may we see the fulness of the Lord's blessing for us, His people, His Church and our lands. May we walk in His blessings and ever take heed to remain there. May we be a generation that fulfils the Lord's call of "If My People".

Blessings in Christ,

Courtney A Laird

PART C: CHARTS & TABLES

If My People

THE CHOSEN PLACE

2 Chronicles 7	1 Kings 18	Acts 2
Temple of Solomon	Mount Carmel	The Upper Room
Solomon	Elijah	The one hundred and twenty gathered as the Church
Great gathering – dedication of the Temple	Great gathering – all Israel assembled	Great gathering – feast of Pentecost
Glory of the Lord filled the House		Upper room filled with a wind from Heaven
Offerings and Sacrifices presented	Sacrifice presented	Living Sacrifices presented
Fire of the Lord	Fire of the Lord	Fire of the Lord
Fire descended	Fire descended	Fire descended
Divine Acceptance	Divine Acceptance	Divine Acceptance
Divine Choice	Divine Choice	Divine Choice
Offerings and Sacrifices consumed	Offering, altar, water and dust consumed	The one hundred and twenty consumed (filled) with the Spirit
Place where prayer was to be offered	Place where prayer was offered	Place where prayer is to be offered
Place where sacrifice was to be offered	Place where sacrifice was offered	Place where living sacrifices are offered
The Chosen Place	The Chosen Place	The Chosen Place
Natural House	Natural Mountain	Spiritual House
The Temple of Solomon – The House of God		The Church – The House of God

THE JUDGEMENTS

2 Chronicles 7	1 Kings 18	Acts 2	Deuteronomy 11
Natural	Natural	Natural and Spiritual	Natural
Shut up heaven that there be no rain – drought	The rains were shut up for three and a half years – Israel was in drought	Natural Drought Spiritual drought of the Spirit and the Word	Shut up heaven that there be no rain
If I command locusts to devour the land – lack of provision	The land was in famine – lack of provision	Natural famine Spiritual famine of the provision of the Word as our daily bread	The land yield not her fruit
Or if I send pestilence	Loss of livestock	Natural death Spiritual death	Ye perish quickly

THE BLESSINGS

2 Chronicles 7	1 Kings 18	Acts 2	Deuteronomy 11
Natural	Natural	Natural and Spiritual	Natural
Rain restored	Rain restored	Outpouring of rain Outpouring of His Spirit and His Word	Rain
Harvest restored	Famine ended and harvest restored	Harvest of the Word	Harvest
Life restored	Life restored	Life given	Life

SPIRITUAL INCLINE

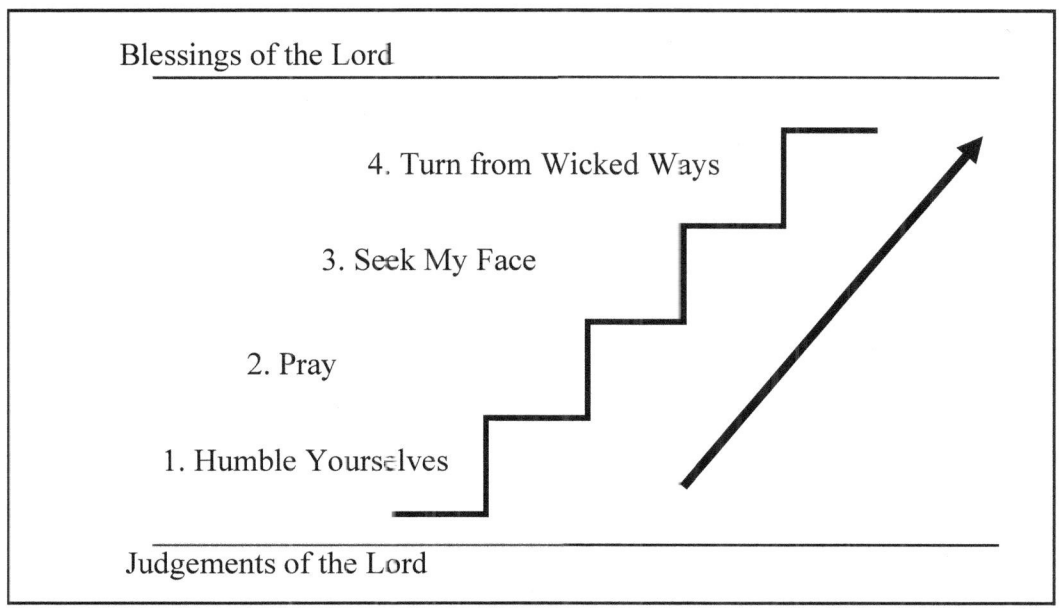

SPIRITUAL DECLINE

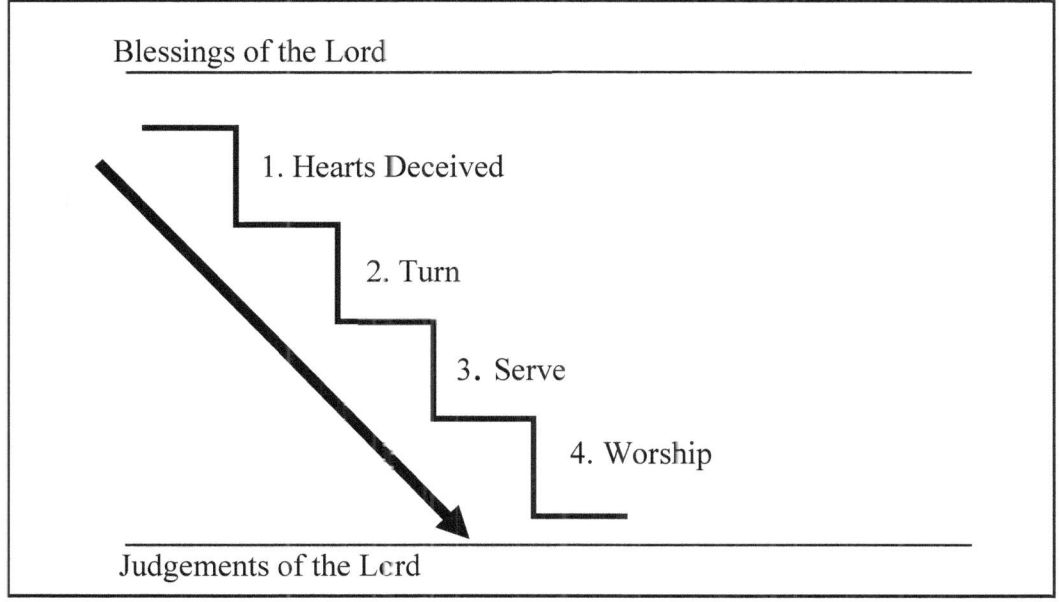

TAKE HEED

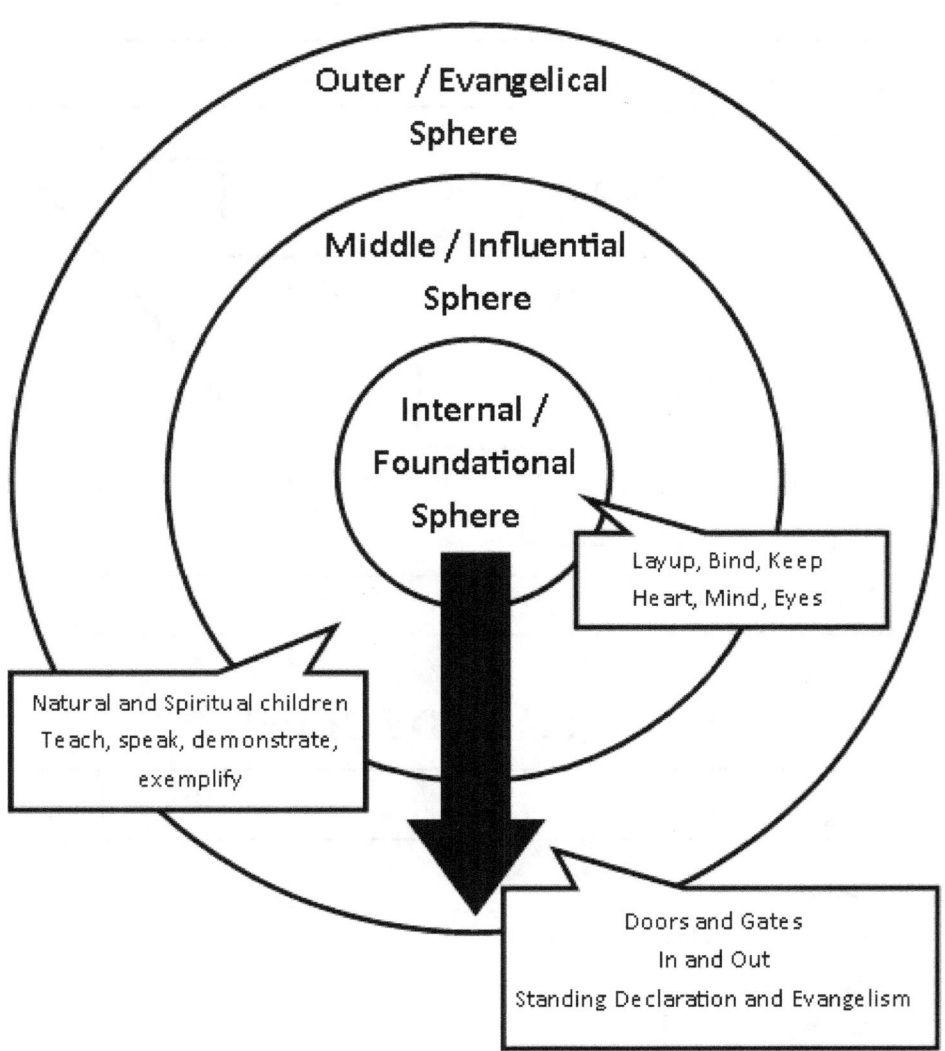

COMBINATION

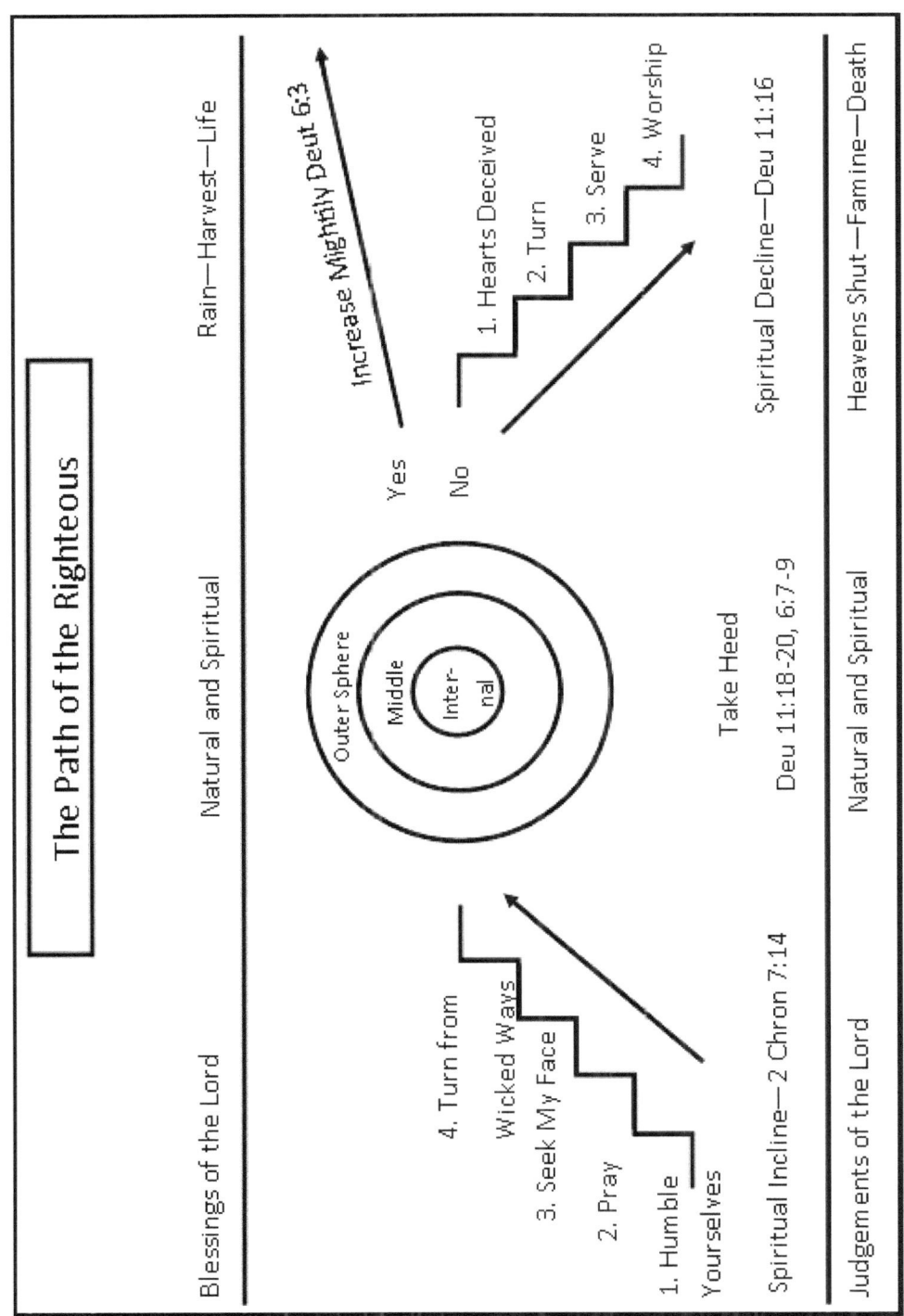

www.ingramcontent.com/pod-product-compliance
Lightning Source LLC
Chambersburg PA
CBHW060533010526
44107CB00059B/2626